SCIENCE,
SCRIPTURE,
and
HOMOSEXUALITY

SCIENCE, SCRIPTURE, and HOMOSEXUALITY

Alice Ogden Bellis and
Terry L. Hufford

THE
PILGRIM
PRESS
Cleveland

To Alice and Glenda, Helen and Sema,
Jim and Sean, and Gregory and Bryce

The Pilgrim Press, 700 Prospect Avenue, Cleveland, Ohio 44115-1100
pilgrimpress.com

Copyright © 2002 by Alice Ogden Bellis and Terry L. Hufford

All rights reserved. Published 2002.

Printed in the United States of America on acid-free paper

08   07   06   05   04   03   02   5   4   3   2   1

Library of Congress Cataloging-in-Publication Data

Bellis, Alice Ogden, 1950-
    Science, scripture, and homosexuality / Alice Ogden Bellis and
Terry L. Hufford.
        p. cm.
    Includes bibliographical references and index.
    ISBN 0-8298-1485-X (alk. paper)
    1. Homosexuality – Religious aspects – Christianity. 2. Homo-
sexuality – Biblical teaching. I. Hufford, Terry L.   II. Title.

BR115.H6 .B45 2002
261.8'35766 – dc21

2001059330

CONTENTS

PREFACE

Science, Scripture, and Homosexuality deals with the problem posed for the Christian community by the growing evidence that homosexuality is at least in part determined genetically, meaning that it occurs naturally within the created order. In contrast, biblical materials depict sexual intercourse between people of the same sex as unnatural. As with controversies of the past when new scientific findings challenged biblical understandings, the emerging scientific findings about homosexuality require an examination of the relevant texts in scripture. Although the next few years will undoubtedly bring forth a more in-depth understanding of the human genome as well as sexual orientation, enough is known already to create a need for this book.

It began as a sabbatical project, but if a book can be compared to a baby, this infant experienced a prolonged period of gestation. One of the difficulties is that Alice Ogden Bellis is a biblical scholar and not a biologist. She took her last biology class in the tenth grade. A lucky turn of fate (or divine providence?) solved that problem. Alice Bellis had been invited to give a presentation in an adult class at Western Presbyterian Church in Washington, D.C., on the Bible and homosexuality. After the presentation, someone introduced her to one of the elders who was in attendance, Terry Hufford, and mentioned that he taught at George Washington University. She asked what he taught and he responded, "biology." At that her ears perked up, not because of this book, but because her daughter was at that very moment taking a course in biology at GW. And so she asked if he was her teacher. He didn't know at that point because it was a very large lecture class, but he was, in fact, her teacher. Although Alice Bellis's daughter had never taken much science and did not think she was very good at it, she did well in Professor Hufford's class.

He is a remarkable teacher, as he transformed Margaret Bellis's intended French major into a double major in biology and French. Not until several months later did it occur to Alice Bellis to approach Professor Hufford about this book. She did, and that's how this baby acquired a father.

We begin with science. In language that is accessible to laypeople, Terry Hufford explains the basics of genetics and the evidence suggesting a physical basis for homosexuality. Much is known scientifically about human sexuality, gender development, and sexual orientation and behavior, and much clearly remains to be known. Human sexuality is determined in three general ways: the genetic makeup of the individual, learned behavior, and environmental influences. Given that human sexuality is in part physiological and in part psychological, saying what level of influence each of these three factors has is a difficult task.

At this time, no "gay gene" is known. Homosexuality is much too complex to result from a single gene, and strong evidence for such a relationship is not currently available. However, this fact does not preclude the possibility of genetic determinants for sexual orientation. As with much of science that seems to contradict a literal reading of the Bible, that conflict is due, in part, to the layperson's misunderstanding or misinterpretation of what the scientists are saying. The conflict also comes, in part, from an attempt to equate scientific statements with biblical statements.

From a faith perspective, biblical statements point to truths that are absolute and dogmatic, although biblical scholars argue that these statements are still open to interpretation. Scientific statements, on the other hand, are probabilistic — they are not absolute, and they are open to modification and change over time as more evidence becomes available. Such a characteristic does not make them weak; in fact, their variability is the strength of science. All scientific statements must be testable and open to the possibility of rejection. A scientific theory is a very powerful statement — one that has been tested over a long period of time and in many different ways — and has not been falsified. Science is clearly the most powerful tool humans have at their disposal for trying to understand natural phenomena.

Our second chapter, authored by Alice Ogden Bellis, deals with the history of the way Christian biblical interpreters have responded to scientific advances that conflicted with a literal reading of the Bible. The episodes covered are the flat earth versus round earth controversy, the geocentric (earth-centered) versus heliocentric (sun-centered) understanding of the relationship between the earth and sun, the conflict over the age of the earth, and Darwinism. Although the last of these episodes is ongoing, the other three have ended with science "winning" over a literal reading of the Bible, although we should not think of scientific and religious interpretations as representative of a battle. Rather, in these cases Christians became convinced that the Bible is authoritative in matters of religion, but not of science, which establishes a principle of interpretation useful in the contemporary consideration of homosexuality. The third chapter looks at other principles of biblical interpretation that are useful in considering scripture passages related to this topic.

The fourth chapter, also authored by Alice Ogden Bellis, examines the biblical evidence relating to homosexuality in light of both traditional principles of biblical interpretation and new scientific findings. Only the antihomosexuality laws in Leviticus are directly applicable out of all the passages from the Hebrew Scriptures sometimes quoted in the debate. These mandates would be considered antiquated along with rules against wearing mixed fibers and the like if it were not for the fact that they may have been in Paul's mind in his letter to the Romans in which he deals briefly with the matter. Since some question persists about the meaning of the relevant words in the two other New Testament passages, Romans 1:26–27 is the crucial passage.

We draw several conclusions regarding these passages.

1. The Bible's negative comments are based on ancient perspectives on human sexuality that contemporary science is rapidly making obsolete.

2. Paul's negative comments about homosexuality are oriented toward the ancient practice of homosexuality, which was

different from the contemporary situation, and therefore his advice cannot be applied unreflectively today.

3. The authors of both the Hebrew Scriptures and the New Testament themselves provide a model for adapting ancient scriptures to contemporary times, including in the most extreme cases jettisoning some sacred traditions.

4. These three options are not alternative approaches to interpretation but instead mutually reinforce each other.

Finding no biblical impediment to same-sex relationships does not automatically mean that all such relationships are sound. The one-flesh metaphor found in Genesis 2:24 ("therefore shall a man leave his father and his mother, and shall cleave unto his wife: and they shall be one flesh," KJV), though often used as a proof text against homosexual partnerships, need not be read this way. The passage expressed the typical arrangement, not the only possible wholesome one. Otherwise how do we explain the fact that both Jeremiah and Jesus were single? The text may suggest that sexual relationships are beneficial beyond the production of children (one nonliteral reading of the metaphor), and that the emotional bonds of intimacy are also valuable (another nonliteral reading of the metaphor). Certainly children were highly desired in the ancient world and often are in the contemporary world, but no interpreter today would want to say that childless couples do not conform to a wholesome pattern of life any more than we would want to say that the single life is inherently wrong. Thus, the Bible may be read as implicitly laying the foundation for philosophical support of sexual relationships of either the heterosexual or homosexual type in which the couple is developing an emotional bond, even if scripture does not explicitly approve such associations.

Homosexuality is a divisive issue. One of the factors leading to negative attitudes is the Bible's stance on the subject. Many Christian denominations refuse to ordain active gays and lesbians and do not permit ministers to officiate at holy union ceremonies. Nevertheless, a sizable minority disagrees with the churches' rulings. We hope that this book makes a contribution to the ongoing debate.

We wish to thank all of the people who over the years contributed to our understanding of this difficult issue and encouraged us to bring this baby to birth — our students and colleagues, pastors and church members, and our families and friends. Special thanks go to our editor at the Pilgrim Press, George R. Graham, who believed in this book and helped make it a reality.

	Cause	Bible
Alcoholism:	Gene/predis	Sin if act on it
Homosexuality:	Gene/pred	unknown

SCIENCE, SEXUAL ORIENTATION, AND THE CHRISTIAN COMMUNITY

The topic of homosexuality has generated a significant emotional response from some individuals, particularly from people within the religious community. That response has largely been negative, characterizing homosexuality as a degenerative sickness, a mental disorder, unethical, immoral, unnatural, a depravity, and an abomination. By others homosexuality has been viewed as a gift from God. Reaction to same-sex attraction involves values, social experiences, personal interpretation, and "natural" affinities having religious, legal, social, and medical (scientific) underpinnings. In this chapter, we focus on scientific research regarding homosexuality, but we also must realize that social and cultural values have influenced the way that science has approached this issue.

Present sociological and personal views toward homosexuality have their origins in prehistory and are based on a biological imperative. Short life spans (thirty years or less on average by some estimates) and high rates of infant mortality characterized early human life.[1] Some writers think that for the first one thousand years or so of human existence, the average life span may have been around fifteen to seventeen years.[2] During the sixteenth, seventeenth, and eighteenth centuries, the mean life span was

---

1. See E. L. Simons, "Human Origins," *Science* 245 (1989): 1343–50; D. W. E. Smith, *Human Longevity* (Oxford: Oxford University Press, 1993), 11.

2. Smith, *Human Longevity,* 12.

still only about thirty years. However, an individual who survived that long had a good probability of surviving for another thirty years.[3] Thus, procreation would have been not only important but essential to the continuing existence of the society. Understanding why preferential and exclusive homosexuality would be viewed in an extremely negative way is not difficult. Such behavior would clearly not result in the birth of children and would therefore be highly detrimental to the very existence of the community. The importance of childbirth became, for some, an underlying principle that gave rise to doctrine in early Christianity. St. Ambrose is said to have stated, "The child is the only reason for a woman to marry."[4] Augustine said, "The good of marriage, therefore, among all nations and peoples lies in the purpose of procreation and in faithful preservation of chastity."[5]

Information available regarding the prehistory of sexual behavior is not well known. However, from the biological perspective, it is highly likely that the earliest humans engaged in certain sexual practices that today we might consider to be homosexual. The pygmy chimps, or bonobos, represent a well-documented instance of homosexual activity among the great apes.[6] Taylor writes, "As soon as there were written records, from around 5,000 years ago in the Near East, we find references to many of the sexual practices — homosexuality, male and female transsexualism and transvestitism, masturbation — familiar to us today."[7] He also states that homosexual activity was widespread in me-

---

3. See M. A. Vinovskis, "The 1789 Life Table of Edward Wigglesworth," *Journal of Economic History* 31 (1971): 579–90; P. Laslett, "Societal Development and Aging," in *Handbook of Aging and the Social Sciences,* ed. R. H. Binstock and E. Shanas (New York: Van Nostrand Reinhold, 1985), 199–230; J. E. Knodel, *Demographic Behavior of the Past* (Cambridge: Cambridge University Press, 1988).

4. As quoted in P. Erdokimov, *The Sacrament of Love: The Nuptial Mystery in the Light of the Orthodox Tradition,* trans. A. P. Gythiel and V. Steadman (Crestwood, N.Y.: St. Vladimir's Seminary Press, 1985), 22.

5. Augustine, *The Good of Marriage,* partially translated in *Marriage in the Early Church,* ed. and trans. David G. Hunter, Sources of Early Christian Thought (Minneapolis: Augsburg Fortress, 1992), 120–21.

6. See, for example, T. Taylor, *The Prehistory of Sex* (New York: Bantam Books, 1996), 80–81.

7. Ibid., 182.

dieval monasteries and that the segregation of women within the medieval castle would have led to lesbian liaisons.[8] Researchers and writers generally express that homosexuality exists in all cultures, but that statement is hard to document. In the history of many cultures, finding ritualistic events in which an individual of one sex is considered to represent the opposite sex is not uncommon. Thus, any sexual activity between them and an "actual" member of their sex would not be considered homosexual by members of their community. In certain cultures, entrance into a kind of homosexual relationship was not unusual for a young man or young woman.[9] A substantial body of Greek literature describes homosexual relationships between youth and older men. Plutarch expressed the opinion that the only true form of love was that between a man and his youth.[10] The Roman world also acknowledged homosexual behavior.[11] Throughout history, sociological, political, and religious tolerance or acceptance of homosexual behavior has varied.

Even within the Christian community, homosexuality, particularly before the late Middle Ages, was widely tolerated or simply ignored. Christian ceremonies for the union of male partners persisted in Eastern Europe into the twentieth century.[12] Twelfth-century poet Bernard of Morlas wrote that gay people were "as common as grains of barley in harvest, as oysters in the sea or sands in the shore."[13] That view changed dramatically with the writings of Thomas Aquinas. E. F. Rogers Jr. offers an excellent discussion of the writings of Aquinas and various interpretations of them.[14]

8. Ibid., 222.

9. See, for example, S. P. Ramet, ed., *Gender Reversals and Gender Cultures* (New York: Routledge, 1996).

10. As quoted in R. Miles, *The Women's History of the World* (New York: Harper Trade, 1990), 68.

11. S. Coote, ed., *The Penguin Book of Homosexual Verse* (New York: Viking Penguin, 1987), 33.

12. J. Boswell, *Christianity, Social Tolerance, and Homosexuality: Gay People in Western Europe from the Beginning of the Christian Era to the Fourteenth Century* (Chicago: University of Chicago Press, 1980), 173.

13. As quoted in Coote, *The Penguin Book of Homosexual Verse,* 118.

14. E. F. Rogers Jr., *Sexuality and the Christian Body: Their Way into the Triune God* (Oxford: Blackwell, 1999).

Homosexuality remains an issue of major concern, as is evident simply by accessing the World Wide Web. Literally thousands of files are available, some scientific and professing to be unbiased, most strongly biased by the prejudices of the writer (both positively and negatively). A few sources test the limits of personal expression.

Given that current societal views have, to some degree, emerged out of biological considerations, does biology have any value in providing guidance in our considerations of homosexuality? Unfortunately, unequivocal scientific data concerning homosexuality is not widely available. The existing data must be considered in a cautious and critical manner.

How does the nonbiologist make any sense out of what, in many instances, seems to be conflicting scientific data? Adding to the confusion are articles written by individuals who, one would suppose, have a scientific background and therefore a degree of expertise. These articles, written primarily by M.D.s and occasionally by Ph.D.s, often take a very negative view of results obtained through scientific studies of homosexuality. In addition, certain professionals in the field of psychology (often classified as a social science) dispute the scientific findings and present conflicting opinions. To many people in our society, the opinions and findings of the social scientist and the natural scientist would be equally respected in consideration of humanity.

The question before us, then, is how can one interpret the results of biological studies on homosexuality? To adequately interpret these studies, several questions need answers. Is homosexuality a conscious choice or a genetic condition? Is it a learned behavior or is it innate (that is, wholly genetic)? Is the condition primarily the result of nurture (environmental influences) or nature (genetic influences)? If genetic, is the condition to be considered an anomaly, an abnormality, or simply an alternative expression of sexuality?

We can attempt to answer some of these questions through consideration of the evidence available. In so doing, we need to consider five principal issues:

- The definition of homosexuality and the kind or kinds of behavior that characterize it
- Appropriate scientific methodology
- Appropriate and adequate sampling
- The scientists' view of "truth"
- The relationship of environment and genetics on human characteristics and behavior

Karl Maria Kertbeny (in private correspondence in 1868) is considered the source for the term "homosexual." The word first appeared in print in two anonymous German pamphlets written in 1869, and Charles Gilbert Chaddock introduced it into the English language in 1892.[15] In general, the term signifies a sexual attraction to members of the same gender. To some, this term can refer to either sexual feelings toward members of one's own gender or sexual practices with members of one's own gender. Others would argue that two different terms should be employed: "homoerotic" in reference to feelings and "homosexual" in reference to practices. Meyer-Bahlburg summarized the classical view of homosexuality in 1984 as he recounted the writing of a German lawyer and writer named Ulrichs. In a letter written to relatives in 1862, Ulrichs described the differentiation of the external genitalia in male and female embryos and the origin of genital intersexes. Ulrichs continues in his Memnon of 1868 to describe a Uraniern, that is a homosexual, as having the soul of a woman innate in a male body.[16]

Given that either feeling or acts can be considered to characterize homosexuality, identification or characterization of a "homosexual" can therefore be questioned. This consideration becomes important when one reviews studies of "homosexuals" versus "heterosexuals." Does the researcher consider an individual to be a homosexual because they identify themselves as

---

15. D. M. Halperin, *One Hundred Years of Homosexuality* (New York: Routledge, 1990), 15.

16. H. F. L. Mayer-Bahlburg, "Psychoendocrine Research on Sexual Orientation: Current Status and Future Options," *Progress in Brain Research* 61 (1984): 375.

a homosexual, because other individuals term the individual a homosexual, or because, based on certain criteria developed by the researcher, the researcher determines the subject to be a homosexual? How does one classify people who rather indiscriminately have sex with both genders? Obviously any of these methods can introduce sampling error, as all require a particular view of what constitutes homosexuality. This question becomes particularly significant as one considers the question of homosexuality as a genetic condition. If, for example, an individual has never engaged in a homosexual act yet has erotic feelings toward other members of his or her own gender, could one expect that person's genetic makeup to be similar to another person's who has those same feelings and has actually acted on them and engaged in homosexual acts? Society would generally consider the latter to be a homosexual, but not the former.

The Importance of Methodology and Sampling

Methodology is particularly significant to any scientific investigation. In certain of the reports we consider, the specific question asked was: "Does homosexuality have a scientific basis?" If so, then homosexuals should differ biologically in some way from heterosexuals. Thus, whether the investigator is interested in conducting a DNA linkage analysis, looking at the size of a group of cells in the hypothalamus, or considering the size of the anterior commissure in the brain, one way to approach such research would be in the form of a null hypothesis. A null hypothesis would state that no difference exists between homosexuals and heterosexuals for the particular condition being studied. Whether the investigator is making a null hypothesis or a hypothesis that states the homosexual differs in some specific way from the heterosexual, the purpose of testing is an attempt to disprove that hypothesis. A hypothesis that cannot be disproven is tentatively accepted. To be examined scientifically, a question must be subject to review and possible rejection. Also, the results obtained must be repeatable; that is, an investigator who repeats the study dozens of times using the same procedures and under the same conditions should obtain essentially the same results. In addition, these results must be replicable; other investigators using the same approach and conditions as the first should also obtain the same results. Thus, repeatability and replicability are essential to valid scientific findings.

A significant, yet somewhat separate, aspect of methodology is the sampling program. Validity and adequacy of sampling has an impact on the reliability of results. In the collection of quantifiable data, analyzing those data statistically is important, requiring that a statistical tool be selected and the analysis be carried out in such a way that the results are appropriate to the statistical test employed. Each different statistical test has its own particular underlying requirements. To be valid, data must be in a form appropriate to the statistical test being used. In addition, any statistical test requires a particular sample size for validity. In general, with a larger sample size, one can place more faith in the results. With a small sample size, chance errors have a greater significance — that is, with a small sample size the probability greatly increases of a variation being caused by chance error rather than an inherent real difference in the data.

Another criterion involves the way in which the investigator establishes the control and test groups. If, for example, the homosexual group chosen for study was selected from a population of individuals with AIDS, how can one interpret any differences from the control group that might be found? The difference could have been due to the influence of AIDS, or perhaps a condition associated with the homosexuality. Likewise, if the test group is chosen from among individuals undergoing psychological counseling, the same kind of difficulty exists.

If a biological study is carried out in an appropriate fashion, what do the inferences drawn from the obtained result mean? The nonscientist likes to know what is "true." "Truth" is generally thought of as that which can be believed. To others, however, the term "truth" is that which is revealed. God is truth; thus, God's word — the Bible — is truth. As God can deal with nothing but truth, truth is absolute. Statements that seem to reflect God's thinking are thus stated dogmatically. They have no alternative.

To scientists, dogmatism is the antithesis to their way of thinking. Nothing is absolute; everything is tentative. That which the biologist accepts as truth today may be disproven tomorrow. To the biologist, truth is probabilistic, that which, given the evidence available, is most likely to be an appropriate explanation. A good biologist does not say, "This is what happens," but instead says, "This is what I think happens given the evidence available to me."

Finally, how are we to understand the impact of heredity on human behavior? Obviously, many years of study are required to begin to understand all the mechanisms and implications of human genetics. The reader cannot become knowledgeable about all these aspects in this brief publication. Certain knowledge, however, is essential to making any sense out of recent genetic research that might reflect on our understanding of homosexuality.

Understanding Human Genetics

Each human has forty-six pairs of structures called chromosomes that reside within the nucleus of most cells of the body. (Some cells, however, are enucleate — that is, they have no nucleus — while others may be polynucleate and thus have double the number of chromosomes.) The individual obtains one of each kind of chromosome from the father, another of each kind from the mother. Of those forty-six pairs, forty-five are termed somatic chromosomes and are found in the nuclei of both the male and female cells. The forty-sixth pair differs in male and female and thus is termed the sex chromosome. The term "sex chromosome" simply means that this pair differs in the two sexes, not that this pair controls sexuality in humans. Certainly, many of the genes associated with sexuality reside in these chromosomes, termed the X and Y in the male (the female has only one kind of sex chromosome, the X), but other genes reside in somatic — the nonsex — chromosomes.

"Gene" is a rather vague term that over the years has been described in many different ways. This work does not enter into a detailed discussion of genes. For our purposes here, a gene represents a specific region of biochemical code associated with a chromosome. That code is translated in the cell as a specific polypeptide, which in turn participates in forming a protein of the cell. These proteins are significant as building blocks and as enzymes. The enzymes of the cell are ultimately responsible for all biochemical reactions that take place there. Thus, the enzymes, and indirectly the genes, are at least partly responsible for all that happens in a cell: its development, appearance, and activities. The genes can be thought of as conditioners for development, establishing potentiality for the individual. Environment, however, is the determiner of development. Environment, both internal and external, controls whether a gene is turned on (is functional) or turned off, and environment influences the degree of expressivity of the gene.

Many people understand inheritance based on the work of Gregor Mendel. Mendel worked with the garden pea and carefully selected characteristics that were influenced by a single gene (although he had no idea such things existed). The gene (for him, the characteristic) had two and only two alternate expressions, and depending on which of the alternative traits, or alleles, of the gene were present in the individual, the character expressed was either one or the other. No additional alternative expressions were available. Certain human characteristics fall into this pattern. Others are non-Mendelian but exhibit the same general pattern in having two and only two expressions; they differ in being present in different ratios in male and female. Such a trait is referred to as sex-linked, that is, borne on the X or Y chromosome.

An example of an X-linked trait is hemophilia. Hemophilia is due to the presence of a recessive gene. A recessive gene is one that is expressed only in the absence of its dominant allele. Given that a female has two X-chromosomes, two recessive alleles must be present if the individual is to be a hemophiliac. The male, however, has only a single X chromosome; thus only a single recessive allele is required for hemophilia to occur. In a family where the father is normal — that is, carries the dominant allele in his X chromosome — and the mother is a carrier (with one dominant allele and one recessive allele), the male children have a 50 percent probability of being hemophilic while the female children have no chance of being hemophilic.

Humans exhibit many other patterns of inheritance. Some patterns are controlled by many alleles for a single gene, with many different expressions occurring for the same gene. Multiple genes control others; that is, many different genes influence the same character. Some genes are epistatic in nature; one gene interferes in some way with the expression of a second gene. Other genes are linked, inherited together, so that when one trait is present in an individual the second trait generally is also present. Genes in humans can be redundant; the same gene can be found in different chromosomes. Other genes can be pleiomorphic, a single gene that may produce many different effects. These examples represent only some of the complexity associated with human inheritance.

I have used the term "expressivity" several times to refer to the degree to which a particular condition exists. For example, one might consider the presence or absence of freckles to be controlled by a single gene. An allele of that gene may result in the individual having no freckles while the alternate allele produces freckles. Yet, some individuals have only a few freckles while others may have many. In this instance, the gene has expressed itself differently in different individuals.

A second important term to consider is penetrance. Penetrance is expressed in proportionality and refers to the frequency at which a gene is expressed when present. Some people believe that if an individual has a particular gene, the trait associated with that gene always appears, but that belief is in error. If the gene always appeared, one would say that the particular gene was 100 percent penetrant. If a gene were never expressed when present in the individual, its penetrance would be 0 percent. Most genes are penetrant at 50 percent or above. The significance of this understanding is obvious.

As an example, many genes are being identified as a result of the Human Genome Project, and certain of them are now specifically linked with particular diseases. Let us suggest that as the result of a screening analysis, an individual is told she has the gene linked with a particular disease. The individual might immediately assume she is doomed to contract the dreaded disease. In fact, she may not, and the probability of getting the disease or not getting the disease is based, at least in part, on the degree of penetrance of that gene. A second factor, and one that will be considered later in more depth, is the effect of environment on the outcome. A third factor may be the presence or absence of a second, epistatic gene in the individual that could influence the expression of the first.

Genetic Research

With this basic understanding of the scientific process and some knowledge of genetics, we are ready to examine some of the research findings related to homosexuality. Perhaps the most widely discussed studies are those of Hamer et al. that appeared in the journal *Science.* In 1992, Hamer and his group discovered that thirty-three of forty gay males shared a genetic mutation in a small region of the X chromosome.[17] Hamer referred to this region of the chromosome as Xq28. In a later study, DNA linkage analysis established a link between the Xq28 marker and sexual orientation in males but not in females.[18] Hamer carefully pointed out that his results indicated a region on a chromosome and not a single gene (the region was large enough to contain several hundred genes); the region was correlated with homosexuality in males but wasn't necessarily a determinant for it; the underlying mechanism for inheritance of the mutation was unknown; and the study needed replicating.[19] In spite of these cautions, certain members of the press began to make reference to the "gay gene."

Given that Hamer identified Xq28 as a region — not a gene,

17. D. H. Hamer, S. Hu, V. L. Magnuson, N. Hu, and A. M. L. Pattatucci, "A Linkage between DNA Markers on the X Chromosome and Male Sexual Orientation," *Science* 261 (1993): 324.

18. S. Hu, A. M. Pattatucci, C. Patterson, L. Li, D. W. Fulker, S. S. Cherny, L. Kruglyak, and D. H. Hamer, "Linkage between Sexual Orientation and Chromosome Xq28 in Males but Not in Females," *Nature Genetics* 11 (1995): 252.

19. Hamer et al., "A Linkage between DNA Markers on the X Chromosome and Male Sexual Orientation," 325–26.

as reported by many journalists and other writers — reference to a "gay gene" is not consistent with the actual research findings, which suggest that some sequence of DNA within the Xq28 region may constitute a gene for homosexuality. In addition, the concept of an X-linked gene that influences homosexual behavior is fraught with difficulties. A major problem is the inheritance pattern itself. As male offspring derive their X chromosome from their mother, the concept suggests that a mother, heterosexual in orientation, might be the carrier for the homosexual gene. (Another suggestion is that the gene is recessive.) The consequences of this outcome would, like the hemophilia example given earlier, result in the probability of one-half of her male offspring being homosexual. The finding would also suggest that none of her female offspring would be homosexual, if we assumed the father to be heterosexual. Hamer's studies with Pattatucci[20] and with Hu et al.[21] would seem to support this idea. However, Hamer's studies do not carefully trace homosexuality through the mother's side of the family; thus arriving at any conclusions regarding the mechanism for inheritance is somewhat difficult. A second difficulty with the research is one of sampling and goes back to an earlier question regarding the characterization of homosexuality. The individuals were self-acknowledged homosexual men and their families.

Perhaps a more significant argument is the assumption that a single gene can produce homosexual behavior. That such a complex behavior pattern, even if genetically based, could possibly be due to a single gene is highly unlikely. Such complex patterns in humans, for which some knowledge of their genetic derivation is known, have been due to clusters of genes.[22] Sev-

---

20. A. M. L. Pattatucci and D. H. Hamer, "Development and Familiality of Sexual Orientation in Females," *Behavioral Genetics* 25 (1994): 407–20.

21. S. Hu et al., "Linkage between Sexual Orientation and Chromosome Xq28 in Males but Not in Females," 253.

22. See J. M. Hettema, C. A. Prescott, and K. S. Kendler, "A Population-Based Twin Study of Generalized Anxiety Disorder in Men and Women," *Journal of Nervous and Mental Disorder* 189 (2001): 413–20; M. J. Meaney, "Maternal Care, Gene Expression, and the Transmission of Individual Differences in Stress Reactivity Across Generations," *Annual Review of Neuroscience* 24 (2001): 1161–92; R. Plomin, J. C. DeFries, G. E. McClearn, and P. McGuffin, *Behavioral Genetics* (New York: Worth

eral authors have specifically suggested that homosexuality is polygenic.[23]

In 1995 Hamer was reported under investigation by the Office of Research Integrity, an arm of the Department of Health and Human Services, regarding the 1993 research. A postdoctoral fellow in Hamer's lab apparently reported that his independent examination of Hamer's data indicated that information had been left out of the report that may have weakened the statistical significance of Hamer's findings.[24] In addition, an independent effort by George Ebers, a neurogeneticist at the University of Western Ontario and an expert on multiple sclerosis, to duplicate Hamer's work reportedly failed. Ebers reported to have found no evidence whatsoever for a genetic link to homosexuality.[25] The ability to duplicate findings, as mentioned earlier, is one of the keystones to validating scientific inquiry. Hamer, in rebuttal, states that he never said there was a "gay gene," but rather that genes play a role in the development of homosexuality. Hamer further states that he was able to confirm his results in a second study.[26]

Concordance Studies

Another source of evidence for inheritance of sexual orientation comes from what has been termed concordance studies. "Concordance" means sameness with regard to the inheritance of a particular characteristic. If the characteristic in question is homosexuality, and one is conducting a study of identical twins, a

Publishers, 2001), 449; P. L. Roubertoux, "What Can the Neurobiologist Learn from Mapping Genes Linked with Behavioral Traits?" *Behavioral Genetics* 31 (2001): 104.

23. C. E. Waddell, "The Heterogeneity of Homosexuality," *Medical Journal of Australia* 58 (1993): 70; E. M. Miller, "Homosexuality, Birth Order, and Evolution: Toward an Equilibrium Reproductive Economics of Homosexuality," *Archives of Sexual Behavior* 29 (2000): 1–34.

24. S. Lehrman, " 'Gay Gene' Study under Scrutiny: Scientist Investigated for Misconduct," *San Francisco Examiner,* July 7, 1995, A-1.

25. G. Ebers, "Male Homosexuality: Absence of Linkage to Microsatellite Markers at Xq28," *Science* 284 (1999): 665–67.

26. S. Hu et al, "Linkage between Sexual Orientation and Chromosome Xq28 in Males but Not in Females," 248–56.

concordance rate of 100 percent would indicate that in every instance where one twin is homosexual, the other twin is also homosexual. Kallmann found nearly 100 percent concordance for homosexuality in male identical twins and 16 percent concordance for male fraternal twins.[27] This finding, if taken at face value, would seem to provide strong evidence for a genetic link to homosexuality. (The percentage of individuals in the general population who are exclusively homosexual has variously been reported between 2 and 10 percent.) However, one needs to consider the source of the sample. Kallman's study was drawn primarily from institutionalized mentally ill patients. Schlegel, some ten years later, found similar high concordance in his study of 113 twin pairs, reporting 95 percent concordance for homosexuality in monozygotic (identical) twins and 5 percent concordance in dizygotic (fraternal) twins.[28] Again, taken at face value, these results would represent strong support for the concept of a genetic basis for homosexuality. Dizygotic twins are just as genetically different from one another as are nontwin brothers and sisters; thus the high concordance rate for monozygotic twins and the low concordance rate for dizygotic twins is quite revealing. This study has an adequate simple size, but some investigators have seriously questioned the methodology.

Bailey and Pillard conducted a large study and reported that for male identical twins raised together, the concordance rate was 52 percent. This figure dropped to 22 percent concordance for nonidentical twins raised together, and to approximately 10 percent for nontwin siblings or an adopted brother raised together. These data would also point to a strong genetic factor.[29] The problem of small sample size was largely eliminated in the study; the sample included 56 pairs of identical twins, 54 pairs of fraternal twins, 142 nontwin siblings, and 57 pairs of adoptive brothers. Again,

27. F. J. Kallmann, "Comparative Twin Study on the Genetic Aspects of Male Homosexuality," *Journal of Nervous and Mental Disorder* 115 (April 1952): 290.

28. W. W. Schlegel, "Die Konstitutionsbiologischen Grundagen der homosexualität," *Zeitschrift für Menschliche Vererbungs- und Konstitutionslehre* 36 (1962): 354.

29. J. M. Bailey and R. Pillard, "A Genetic Study of Male Sexual Orientation," *Archives of General Psychiatry* 48 (1991): 1092.

the aspect of sample selection can be questioned. Was the sample selected in an entirely random fashion? Examination would indicate that it was not, as the participants were recruited through ads placed in homosexual publications. Another study, by King and McDonald, reported the results of a much smaller number of participants (38 males, 8 females). King and McDonald reported a 25 percent concordance rate among monozygotic twins and a 12 percent concordance rate among dizygotic twins. Overall, 20 percent of the respondents reported that their co-twin was also homosexual.[30] The results are somewhat difficult to interpret as the study is not clear as to whether the respondent and co-twin were exclusively homosexual or if they were bisexual. King and McDonald also recruited through ads placed in several local and national "gay" periodicals. Their study can be faulted too on the basis of small sample size and no confirmatory information regarding the sexual orientation of the co-twin.

Whitman, Diamond, and Martin found a 64.7 percent concordance rate for 34 pairs of male monozygotic twins. They characterized 5.9 percent of the pairs to be partially concordant (showing a disparity of two to three points on the six-point Kinsey scale of sexual orientation).[31] Thus, 29.4 percent of the pairs were discordant (that is, one was homosexual, the other was not). Among monozygotic female twins (only 4 pairs were included in the study), 75 percent were concordant and 25 percent discordant. Among the dizygotic twins, 4 pairs of male/male twins were concordant and 10 pairs were discordant; 3 pairs of male/female twins were concordant, 2 pairs were partially concordant, and 4 pairs were discordant.[32] Gasztonyi studied the family trees of 16 homosexual males. He found the familial cluster of three cases corresponded to the X-linked recessive in-

30. M. King and E. McDonald, "Homosexuals Who Are Twins: A Study of 46 Probands," *British Journal of Psychiatry* 160 (1992): 408.

31. A. C. Kinsey, W. B. Pomeroy, and C. E. Martin, *Sexual Behavior in the Human Male* (Philadelphia: W. B. Saunders, 1948), 651.

32. F. L. Whitman, M. Diamond, and J. Martin, "Homosexual Orientation in Twins: A Report on 61 Pairs and Three Triplet Sets," *Archives of Sexual Behavior* 22 (1993): 193.

heritance. In reviewing the results of family, twin, and adoption studies, and the recent findings of molecular genetic and brain research, Gasztonyi concluded that male homosexuality comprises different subgroups, but one major entity is caused by X-linked recessive gene(s). He concluded that this genetic background represents a predisposition that is triggered or suppressed by external factors.[33]

If homosexuality is genetically determined, why would concordance not always be 100 percent for identical twins? As they come from the same zygote, should they not be identical in every respect? Actually, many factors act upon developing embryos that influence developmental patterns, even in two embryos derived from the same zygote. The complexity of such gene interaction, which is both biochemical and environmental in nature, is beyond the scope of this report. A second interesting observation is the 22 percent concordance for nonidentical twins raised together, as reported in the Bailey and Pillard study.[34] Genetically, nonidentical twins are no more similar to each other than they are to other nontwin siblings. In addition, concordance for both nontwin siblings and for adoptive brothers (who would be expected to be quite different genetically) is higher than might be expected purely by chance. These data indicate a significant environmental influence. Bailey, Pillard, and others conducted a similar study with female identical twins raised in the same family and found that where one twin identified herself as lesbian, 48 percent of the time the other member also said she was homosexual.[35] These data can indicate one of two things; either the inheritance pattern is not sex-linked or environmental influences are of major significance in sexual orientation. In addition, one needs to be aware of the numerous studies that report largely conflicting results, indicating a high degree of discordance among monozygotic

33. Z. Gasztonyi, "Genetic Evaluation of Male Homosexuality," *Orv Hetil* 139 (1998): 247–49.

34. Bailey and Pillard, "A Genetic Study of Male Sexual Orientation," 1093.

35. J. M. Bailey, R. C. Pillard, M. C. Neale, and Y. Agyei, "Heritable Factors Influence Sexual Orientation in Women," *Archives of General Psychiatry* 50 (1993): 219.

twins.[36] Unfortunately, all of these studies are suspect because of the small numbers of individuals sampled.

If environmental influences are in fact of major significance, studies of monozygotic twins raised apart from one another would seem to be informative. Unfortunately, few such studies are available, and those studies reported have sample sizes too small to yield significant results. A major workshop, the Dahlem Workshop held in Berlin in 1992, had as its principal focus *Twins as a Tool of Behavioral Genetics*. The aspect of sexual orientation was not considered at these week-long meetings. Whitman, Diamond, and Martin included in their study only two pairs of twins reared apart. One pair exhibited concordance in sexual orientation, the other pair discordance.[37] These authors cite the work of Bouchard et al. and state that of the more than one hundred sets of reared-apart twins observed in that study, five sets were homosexual monozygotic twins. However, while Bouchard et al. state that they included sexual life history interviews as part of their study, their report actually makes no reference to the issue of homosexuality.[38]

Green reports on research which indicates that 75 percent

36. See J. D. Rainer, A. Mesnikoff, L. C. Kolb, and A. Carr, "Homosexuality and Heterosexuality in Identical Twins," *Psychosomatic Medicine* 22 (1960): 251–59; G. K. Klintworth, "A Pair of Male Monozygotic Twins Discordant for Homosexuality," *Journal of Nervous and Mental Disorder* 135 (1962): 113–25; A. I. Mesnikoff, J. D. Rainer, L. C. Kolb, and A. C. Carr, "Intrafamilial Determinants of Divergent Sexual Behavior in Twins," *American Journal of Psychiatry* 119 (1963): 732–38; N. Parker, "Homosexuality in Twins: A Report on Three Discordant Pairs," *British Journal of Psychiatry* 110 (1964): 489–95; L. L. Heston and J. Shields, "Homosexuality in Twins," *Archives of General Psychiatry* 18 (1968): 149–60; R. Green and R. J. Stoller, "Two Monozygotic (Identical) Twin Pairs Discordant for Gender Identity," *Archives of Sexual Behavior* 1 (1971): 322–26; K. Davidson, H. Brierley, and C. Smith, "A Male Monozygotic Twinship Discordant for Homosexuality," *British Journal of Psychiatry* 118 (1971): 675–82; M. W. Perkins, "Homosexuality in Female Monozygotic Twins," *Behavioral Genetics* 3 (1973): 387–88; R. C. Friedman, F. Wollesen, and R. Trendler, "Psychological Development and Blood Levels of Sex Steroids in Male Identical Twins of Divergent Sexual Orientation," *Journal of Nervous and Mental Disorder* 163 (1976): 283–87; B. Zuger, "Monozygotic Twins Discordant for Homosexuality: Report on a Pair and Significance of the Phenomenon," *Comprehensive Psychiatry Review* 17 (1976): 661–68.
37. Whitman, Diamond, and Martin, "Homosexual Orientation in Twins: A Report on 61 Pairs and Three Triplet Sets," 191–96.
38. T. J. Bouchard, D. T. Lykken, M. McGue, N. L. Segal, and A. Tellegen, "Sources of Human Psychological Differences: The Minnesota Study of Twins Reared Apart," *Science* 250 (1990): 223.

of males who were effeminate as young children became gays as adults.[39] Other studies have correlated lesbianism with the woman's "boyish" behavior as a child.[40] While such studies might suggest that homosexuality is present very early in life and thus is inherited and not learned, these studies are also fraught with difficulties in that they require a stereotyping of what constitutes male or female behavior in children. Even if such behaviors can be categorized in any reliable and valid fashion, a judgment decision still must be made in regard to how much and to what degree "boyish" behavior in female children or "girlish" behavior in male children constitutes a tendency toward homosexuality. These questions are compounded by the degree to which societal, cultural, family, and other environmental influences affect behavior.

Hormonal Studies

Other efforts, which have done little to illuminate the role of genetics in the development of homosexual behavior, include hormonal studies. Given that specific hormones, commonly referred to as sex hormones, in part characterize the male and female, one might suspect these hormones would differ in concentration in the homosexual. This assertion links the aspect of sexual orientation with gender. One's gender is sexually based. During development, hormones play a significant role in gender development. Thus, if we are to consider the possibility that sexual orientation is genetically based, might not hormones also influence it?

In order to have some idea of how and why hormones might or might not influence gender orientation, we need to consider the overall developmental process in humans. Money recognizes

39. R. Green, *The "Sissy Boy Syndrome" and the Development of Homosexuality* (New York: Yale University Press, 1987), 99.
40. G. Phillips and R. Over, "Differences between Heterosexual, Bisexual, and Lesbian Women in Recalled Childhood Experiences," *Archives of Sexual Behavior* 24 (1995): 1–20; Z. Levy, "Sexing the Tomboy," in *Sissies and Tomboys: Gender Nonconformity and Homosexual Childhood,* ed. M. Rottnek (New York: New York University Press, 1999), 180–95.

six (or seven) sex- and gender-related developmental elements as the fertilized egg becomes a sexually mature adult human. These elements are (1) sex chromosome composition, (2) gonadal development, (3) hormone production, (4) development of the genitalia, (5) fetal brain development, (6) assigned gender, and (7) pubertal hormone production. For the sake of simplicity hormone production and development of genitalia can be considered as a single element, phenotypic sex.[41]

Numerous journals and textbooks have discussed the process of fertilization and development.[42] In the production of sperm, an individual sperm nucleus may contain, with its set of somatic chromosomes, either an X sex chromosome or a Y sex chromosome. The female sex chromosomes are only X; thus, when sperm and egg unite, the resulting zygote may be XX or XY, depending upon which sperm entered the egg. The XX chromosome combination typically designates a female, while the XY combination designates a male. Thus, theoretically, sex is determined at the instant of nuclear fusion during the process of fertilization, at the time of production of the zygote nucleus. The significance of the Y chromosome is the presence, on the short arm of that chromosome, of the SRY (**S**ex-determining **R**egion of the **Y**) gene. Approximately seven weeks after fertilization, SRY encodes a transcription factor that triggers conversion of the undifferentiated gonad of the developing embryo to testes. The process by which this occurs is beyond the scope of this text, but in simple terms the process involves the DNA of the SRY region transcribing RNAs which, following an editing process in the nucleus, pass into the cytoplasm of the cells where they are involved in protein production. These proteins (enzymes), in turn, act to trigger the conversion.

Special cells of these developing testes produce a substance called AMH, Anti-Müllerian Hormone, resulting in the disin-

41. J. Money, "The Concept of Gender Identity Disorder in Childhood and Adolescence after 39 Years," *Journal of Sex and Marital Therapy* 20 (1994): 163–77.
42. See, for example, B. M. Carlson, *Human Embryology and Developmental Biology* (St. Louis: Mosby, 1993), 447.

tegration of the Müllerian ducts, which ultimately would have produced the uterus, fallopian tubes, and vagina in the female. Other specialized cells of the developing testes produce testosterone, which stimulates a second set of ducts, the Wolffian ducts, to form the male ducts that ultimately lead from the testes to and through the developing penis. Some of the testosterone is converted to a compound called dihydroxy testosterone (DHT), which cause the conversion of the genital tubercle to the penis, and also cause the development of male glands, such as the prostrate, and the urethra and scrotum.

In the absence of a Y chromosome, no SRY will be present and no AMH will be produced; thus, the Müllerian ducts will develop into the female features mentioned previously. As no male androgens will be produced, the Wolffian ducts will disintegrate and the genital tubercle will develop into the clitoris.

In this developmental process, the sexual differentiation of the rest of the body is clearly affected, not necessarily by the individual's genetics directly, but by the hormones that the gonads secrete. The testicular hormones are crucial for the development of males, and the most important of these, in regard to masculinization of the body, are the androgenic steroids, principally testosterone. If a female receives testosterone at a critical point in development, she will have a completely male exterior.[43] Conversely, if one removes the testes soon after they differentiate, or supplies an androgen blocker, the male will develop a completely female exterior.[44] The ability of a cell to respond to the androgen is based on the presence of an appropriate androgen receptor on the cell's surface, which, in turn, activates a steroid-receptor complex in the cell that binds to the cell's DNA — thereby altering the production of various proteins in the cell. A cell lacking that receptor cannot respond to the androgen. During fetal development both males and females have such receptors on their cell surfaces, but normally only males will produce enough testos-

---

43. S. M. Breedlove, "Sexual Differentiation of the Human Nervous System," *Annual Review of Psychology* 45 (1994): 392.
44. Ibid.

terone to be masculinized. If XX individuals are exposed to higher levels of testosterone, they can be masculinized; if XY individuals have a defective gene for androgen receptors, they are therefore androgen insensitive and feminized.[45] Does the above have any bearing on sexual orientation? A number of studies have primarily been concerned with nonhuman subjects.[46] Those studies concerned with humans have either been inconclusive or have shown no constitutional chemical differences between homosexuals and heterosexuals.[47] Furthermore, in cases where hormonal levels in the adult have been drastically altered through surgical removal of the gonads, sexual shifts have not been induced. Studies conducted on rats have indicated changes in sexual orientation in response to hormonal variations. However, extrapolation of rodent behavioral response to psychological, or even physiological, processes in humans is difficult. Hormonal control mechanisms simply do not operate in the same way in rodent and human.

In regard to fetal brain development, sexual dimorphism of the central nervous system in nonhuman species is well known. Pfaff noted sexual dimorphism in the rat hypothalamus.[48] Raisman and Field pointed out that the preoptic area of female rats had a greater number of a particular class of synapse than did the

45. Ibid., 393–94.
46. See, for example, R. E. Whalen and R. D. Nadler, "Suppression of the Development of Female Mating Behavior by Estradiol Administration in Infancy," *Science* 141 (1963): 273–74; R. F. Mullins and S. Levine, "Hormonal Determinants During Infancy of Adult Sexual Behavior in the Male Rat," *Behavior* 3 (1968): 339–43; S. E. Hendricks, "Influence of Neonatally Administered Hormones and Early Gonadectomy on Rats' Sexual Behavior," *Journal of Comparative and Physiological Psychology* 69 (1969): 408–13; K. Dohler et al., "Pre- and Postnatal Influence of Diethylstilbestrol on Differentiation of the Brain: Neuroanatomical, Neuroendocrine, and Behavioral Evidence," *Progress in Brain Research* 61 (1984): 99–117; F. Naftolin and N. MacLusky, "Aromatization Hypothesis Revisited," in *Differentiation: Basic and Clinical Aspects,* ed. M. Serio (New York: Lippincott-Raven, 1984); R. A. Gorski, "Hormone-induced Sex Differences in Hypothalamic Structure," *Bulletin Tokyo Metropolitan Institute of Neurosciences* 16 (1988): 67–90.
47. G. Dorner et al., "Evocability of a Slight Positive Oestrogen Feedback Action on LH Secretion in Castrated and Oestrogen-primed Men," *Endokrinologie* 66 (1975): 373–76.
48. D. W. Pfaff, "Morphological Changes in the Brains of Adult Male Rats after Neonatal Castration," *Journal of Endocrinology* 36 (1966): 415–16.

preoptic area of males.[49] Nottebohm and Arnold noted prominent sexually dimorphic regions in the brains of songbirds.[50] Sexually dimorphic nuclei were noted in the preoptic area of rats (Gorski et al.), gerbils (Commins and Yahr), guinea pigs (Hines et al.), and ferrets (Tobet et al.).[51] Such studies provide little insight into human sexual orientation. Considered from one perspective, the above studies focus on sexual behavior rather than sexual orientation. Second, sexual behavior in these organisms has a physiological basis while human sexuality is in part physiological, in part psychological. Third, one cannot even assume that the physiology of these organisms is comparable to that of humans; in fact, it likely is not.

Do humans exhibit sexual dimorphism of the central nervous system? Certainly, the brains of the male are larger than those of the female. However, when normalized by body mass, height, or body surface area, that difference largely disappears.[52] Among right-handed individuals, verbal information is more efficiently and effectively processed when presented to the left cerebral hemisphere, while spatial information is better processed when presented to the right cerebral hemisphere. This discrepancy in performance regarding the presentation of information to one

49. G. Raisman and P. M. Field, "Sexual Dimorphism in the Preoptic Area of the Rat," *Science* 173 (1971): 20–22.

50. F. Nottebohm and A. P. Arnold, "Sexual Dimorphism in Vocal Control Areas of the Songbird Brain," *Science* 194 (1976): 211–13.

51. R. A. Gorski, J. H. Gordon, J. E. Shryne, and A. M. Southam, "Evidence for a Morphological Sex Difference within the Medial Preoptic Area of the Rat Brain," *Brain Research* 148 (1978): 333–46; D. Commins and P. Yahr, "Acetyl Cholinesterase Activity in the Sexually Dimorphic Area of the Gerbil Brain: Sex Differences and Influence of Adult Gonadal Steroids," *Journal of Comparative Neurology* 224 (1984): 123–31; M. Hines et al., "Sexually Dimorphic Regions in the Medial Preoptic Area and the Bed Nucleus of the Stria Terminalis of the Guinea Pig Brain: A Description and an Investigation of Their Relationship to Gonadal Steroids in Adulthood," *Journal of Neuroscience* 5 (1985): 40–47; S. A. Tobet, D. J. Zahniser, and M. J. Baum, "Differentiation in Male Ferrets of a Sexually Dimorphic Nucleus of the Preoptic/ Anterior Hypothalamic Area Requires Prenatal Estrogen," *Neuroendocrinology* 44 (1986): 299–308.

52. See D. F. Swaab and M. A. Hoffman, "Sexual Differentiation of the Human Brain: A Historical Perspective," *Progress in Brain Research* 61 (1984): 361–74; M. Peters, "Sex Differences in Human Brain Size and the General Meaning of Differences in Brain Size," *Canadian Journal of Psychology* 45 (1991): 507–22.

side of the brain or the other appears to be greater in males than in females.[53] What this might have to do with sexual orientation, if anything, is unknown. Other studies have reported differences for various regions or structures associated with the brain.[54] None of these characteristics have been shown to specifically differ in homosexual or heterosexual males or females, with one possible exception. Allen and Gorski reported that the anterior commissure (AC), a small tract of axons that communicate between the two cerebral hemispheres, is larger in homosexual men than in heterosexual men.[55] Whether this difference is the result of sexual orientation, the cause of sexual orientation, or has no relationship to sexual orientation has not been conclusively demonstrated.

Neuroanatomic studies, such as Simon LeVay's finding that an area of the hypothalamus (a region of the brain) known as INAH3 is smaller in homosexual men and heterosexual women, are highly questionable.[56] LeVay considered that a likely biological substrate for sexual orientation would be the brain region involved in the regulation of sexual behavior. In nonhuman primates, this region is the medial zone of the anterior hypothalamus. Thus, he directed his attention to the human hypothalamus. A study by Allen et al. suggested that two small groups of neurons

53. S. M. Breedlove, "Sexual Differentiation of the Human Nervous System," *Annual Review of Psychology* 45 (1994): 398.

54. See, for example, J. McGlone, "Sex Differences in Human Brain Asymmetry: A Critical Survey," *Behavioral and Brain Sciences* 3 (1980): 215–63; C. deLacoste and R. Holloway, "Sexual Dimorphism in the Human Corpus Callosum, *Science* 216 (1982): 1431–32; W. Byne, R. Bleier, and L. Houston, "Variations in Human Corpus Callosum Do Not Predict Gender: A Study Using Magnetic Resonance Imaging," *Behavioral Neuroscience* 102 (1988): 222–27; L. Allen et al., "Two Sexually Dimorphic Cell Groups in the Human Brain," *Journal of Neuroscience* 9 (1989): 497–506; S. Clarke et al., "Forms and Measures of Adult and Developing Human Corpus Callosum: Is There Sexual Dimorphism?" *Journal of Comparative Neurology* 280 (1989): 213–30; M. A. Hoffman and D. F. Swaab, "The Sexually Dimorphic Nucleus of the Preoptic Area in the Human Brain: A Comparative Morphometric Study," *Journal of Anatomy* 164 (1989): 55–72.

55. L. S. Allen and R. A. Gorski, "Sexual Orientation and the Size of the Anterior Commissure in the Human Brain," *Proceedings of the National Academy of Sciences* 89 (1992): 7199–7202.

56. S. LeVay, "A Difference in Hypothalamic Structure between Heterosexual and Homosexual Men," *Science* 253 (1991): 1034–37.

(INAH 2 and 3) were significantly larger in men than women.[57] LeVay obtained brain tissue from forty-one subjects at routine autopsies of persons who died at seven metropolitan hospitals in New York and California. Nineteen subjects were homosexual men who died of complications of acquired immunodeficiency syndrome (AIDS). Sixteen subjects were presumed heterosexual women, one of whom died of AIDS. He concluded that INAH 3 did exhibit dimorphism. He found the volume of this nucleus to be more than twice as large in the heterosexual men as in the homosexual men.[58]

A problem with each of these studies is that while the mean value may differ for each group, the standard deviation is quite large, thus making any inference highly questionable. Additionally, each of these studies dealt with a homosexual subgroup consisting largely or totally of individuals who died of AIDS, while the heterosexual subgroup consisted of few who died of AIDS-related causes. The effect of the virus or its treatment on morphology of the hypothalamus or anterior commissure is not known. All the studies cited above have deficiencies. While some may have flawed research design or sampling deficiencies, all are influenced to one degree or another by the lack of consensus on what constitutes homosexuality.

Burr, in his book *A Separate Creation: The Search for the Biological Origins of Sexual Orientation,* cites the view of many researchers that individuals are either homosexual or heterosexual and rejects the concept of bisexuality. As an example, he cites left- and right-handedness and compares it with sexual orientation.[59] While individuals can learn to be ambidextrous, they are not so from birth. Burr is thus suggesting that, in regard to genetic origin, bisexuality is a learned behavior. Not all scientists agree with this contention and believe in the presence of a con-

---

57. L. S. Allen, M. Hines, J. E. Shryne, and R. A. Gorski, "Two Sexually Dimorphic Cell Groups in the Human Brain," *Journal of Neuroscience* 9 (1989): 497.

58. S. LeVay, "A Difference in Hypothalamic Structure between Heterosexual and Homosexual Men," 1035.

59. C. Burr, *A Separate Creation: The Search for the Biological Origins of Sexual Orientation* (New York: Hyperion, 1996), 14–15.

tinuum of behavioral responses from strongly heterosexual to strongly homosexual. As mentioned earlier, these data also suggest a multigene and quantitative model for the inheritance of homosexuality. The concept renders meaningless the search for a homosexual gene.

The Impact of Environment and Interpretation

All the studies cited above are surely influenced to one degree or another by the effect of the environment. Genetics on its own does not determine any developmental or behavioral characteristic. External or internal environmental factors could influence both expression and degree of expression. Yet, such an effect is rarely discussed in the issue of homosexuality. What is the influence of culture, social pressures, parental pressures, and so on? In certain of the twin studies mentioned earlier, discordance can be considered clear indication that something other than genetics is responsible for one twin being heterosexual, the other homosexual.

Finally, one needs to consider the implication of genetically influenced behavior. Scientific learning utilizes a mechanistic approach called reductionism. The scientists develop knowledge of atoms and molecules into knowledge of macromolecular functions such as those of DNA and RNA. This macromolecular knowledge leads to an understanding of the structure and function of cellular organelles and inclusions such as chromosomes, ribosomes, and others, then to cells, tissues, organs, organ systems, and finally to the organism itself. If one wishes to consider higher levels of interaction and ultimately the interaction of the organism to its environment, the study moves to consideration of populations, communities, and ecosystems. This approach, with its narrow focus on one particular level at a time, leads to the development of detailed and specific information. At the same time the investigator can sometimes overlook or forget the limitations that this narrowness of focus imposes.

For example, one might consider an herb growing in a forest, lawn, or garden. While certainly the same plant no matter where it is found, the herb will not look the same in each of the different habitats. It will differ in height, in the shape and size of its leaves, in the characteristics of its stem; even its flowers may look different. In fact, the herb might even develop different reproductive habits and timing. In one habitat, members of the species may show a great deal of uniformity; in another habitat they may exhibit a great deal of diversity. For example, I could split or separate a plant into two separate plants, planting one half in an alpine garden around 6600 feet (2000 meters) above sea level and the other half in my garden (around 106 feet or 32 meters above sea level). The two plants will become very different in their appearance. This remarkable ability of plants with the same genetic makeup to become remarkably different one from the other is called "plasticity." Humans do not exhibit the same degree of plasticity as plants, yet are in the same way influenced by their environment.

During experimentation, the scientist creates conditions under which he can test an untested explanation termed a "hypothesis." The thought or hypothesis thus shapes the experiment, but the nature of the methodology also depends on the skill, wisdom, and creativity of the investigator. Thought and action come together in creative fashion so new dimensions of the phenomenon might be revealed. Thus, while scientists like to give the impression that their experimentation is purely objective, totally separating what is known from what is done is in fact impossible; the experiment entails a mediation of the scientists' understanding of the world. Goethe recognized this dilemma over two hundred years ago. In his *Der Versuch als Vermittler von Object und Subject* ("The Experiment As Mediator between Object and Subject"), he stated:

Thus we can never be too careful in our efforts to avoid drawing hasty conclusions from experiments or using them directly as proof to bear out some theory. For here at this pass, this transition from empirical evidence to judgment, cognition to application, all the inner enemies of man lie in wait: imagination, which sweeps him away on its wings before he knows his feet have left the ground; impatience;

haste; self-satisfaction; rigidity; formalistic thought; prejudice; ease; frivolity; fickleness — this whole theory and its retinue. Here they lie in ambush and surprise not only the active observer but also the contemplative one who appears safe from all passion.... /

I would venture to say that we cannot prove anything by one experiment or even several experiments together, that nothing is more dangerous than the desire to prove some thesis directly through experiments, that the greatest errors have arisen just where the dangers and shortcomings in this method have been overlooked....

Every piece of empirical evidence, every experiment, must be viewed as isolated; yet the human facility of thought forcibly strives to unite all external known objects to it. It is easy to see the risk we run when we try to connect a single bit of evidence with an idea already formed, or use individual experiments to prove some relationship not fully perceptible to the senses but expressed through the creative power of the mind....

Such efforts generally give rise to theories and systems that are a tribute to their author's intelligence. But with undue applause or protracted support they soon begin to hinder and harm the very progress of the human mind they had earlier assisted.

We often find that the more limited the data, the more artful a gifted thinker will become. As though to assert his sovereignty he chooses a few agreeable favorites from the limited number of facts and skillfully marshals the rest so they never contradict him directly. Finally he is able to confuse, entangle, or push aside the opposing facts and reduce the whole to something more like the court of a despot than a freely constituted republic.[60]

A specific example might help inform us concerning the interpretation of scientific results. Koopman et al. were concerned with a

_____

60. D. Miller, trans. and ed., *Goethe: Scientific Studies* (New York: Suhrkamp, 1988), 11–17.

region of the Y chromosome in mice called the sex-determining region or SRY region. If this region determined male sexual characteristics, might it not be possible, they questioned, to turn female mice into male mice by transferring the SRY region into fertilized eggs? They used a technique whereby the SRY region was identified, isolated, and separated from the rest of the DNA in the Y chromosome. That DNA was subjected to a process called DNA amplification whereby the quantity of the DNA is increased. The SRY was then biochemically attached to a specific type of bacterial DNA, called plasmid DNA, through the use of specific enzymes. Under appropriate conditions, some of the SRY DNA became inserted into the plasmid DNA. Such recombinant plasmids were then allowed to be taken up by a growing culture of bacteria, thus resulting in these recombinant plasmids being duplicated and multiplied as their host cell divided and multiplied. This process is termed "cloning," with the bacteria cell producing multiple copies of the mouse DNA as it duplicates its own genome (genetic material).[61]

The next step was to isolate and purify the cloned DNA and inject it into mouse eggs, which was accomplished through a complex process whereby the female mouse is injected with hormones that induce the production of many eggs (superovulation). The females were then mated and one day later the fertilized eggs removed from the oviduct. At this time they are only 100 μm (0.1 mm) in diameter. Within this tiny cell is the nucleus of the sperm. Using a microscope, the investigator injected SRY DNA into the male nucleus prior to its fusion with the egg nucleus. When the two nuclei fuse, fertilization is complete and embryonic development begins.[62]

The fertilized eggs (zygotes) remained in culture overnight. The next day the cultures were examined, and the researcher removed those embryos that had reached the two-cell stage. These embryos were then implanted into previously conditioned female

---

61. P. Koopman, J. Gubbay, N. Vivian, P. Goodfellow, and R. Lovell-Badge, "Male Development of Chromosomally Female Mice Transgenic for SRY," *Nature* 351 (1991): 117.
62. Ibid., 118.

mice. If they implanted properly, a three-week gestation period followed. As a result ninety-three mice were born. DNA from the tissue of each was analyzed to see whether they had taken up the foreign DNA, a condition termed "transgenic." Of the ninety-three, five had become transgenic.[63] Two of the five were normal XY males and exhibited no more masculinity with the extra SRY DNA than those males without it. Two other of the five were normal XX females. Even though both carried the SRY DNA, or male-determining DNA, no sex reversal had taken place. The remaining transgenic mouse was female in regard to chromosome makeup (XX), but male in regard to anatomy and behavior. The testicles were very small; "he" was sterile, yet exhibited completely normal male mouse sexual behavior.[64] The result of this research made the cover of the highly prestigious scientific journal *Nature,* which carried a photograph of the mouse with its testicles clearly visible and the caption, "Making a Male Mouse." The bias was obvious. Had the experiment been featured in a prominent feminist journal, might not the focus have been on the two of three female transgenic mice that behaved as normal females? The headline then might have read "Female Mice Resist Attempt to Make Them into Males"!

Additional Viewpoints

Psychiatrists, psychologists, and sociologists have conducted many studies on the nature and consequences of homosexuality, and the scope of the present publication does not allow discussion of all of these. However, some review might be illuminating. In a Fact Sheet of May 2000 titled *Gay, Lesbian and Bisexual Issues,* the American Psychiatric Association presents the following information: In 1973 the American Psychiatric Association removed homosexuality from its official diagnostic manual, *The Diagnostic and Statistical Manual of Mental Disorders, Second Edition (DSM II).* Review of the literature available and consultation with experts in the

---

63. Ibid.
64. Ibid., 119.

field led APA's Board of Trustees to determine that homosexuality does not meet the criteria to be considered a mental illness. In addition, the APA stated that, to date, no replicated scientific studies supported any specific biological etiology for homosexuality. Similarly, no specific psychosocial or family dynamic cause for homosexuality has been identified, including histories of childhood sexual abuse.[65] In *DSM-III,* published in 1987, ego-dystonic homosexuality was not included after a similar review. An APA 1997 Fact Sheet on Homosexual and Bisexual Issues states that no published scientific evidence supports the efficacy of reparative therapy as a treatment to change one's sexual orientation.[66] In 1992, the American Psychiatric Association, recognizing the power of the stigma against homosexuality, issued the following statement:

> Whereas homosexuality per se implies no impairment in judgment, stability, reliability, or general social or vocational capabilities, the American Psychiatric Association calls on all international health organizations, and individual psychiatrists in other countries, to urge the repeal in their own country of legislation that penalizes homosexual acts by consenting adults in private. And further, the APA calls on these organizations and individuals to do all that is possible to decrease the stigma related to homosexuality wherever and whenever it may occur.[67]

In 1975 the American Psychological Association issued a statement on homosexuality. The opening paragraphs of that statement read as follows:

> The research on homosexuality is very clear. Homosexuality is neither mental illness nor moral depravity. It is simply a way a minority of our population expresses human love and sexuality. Study after study documents the mental health of

---

65. American Psychiatric Association, *Fact Sheet of the American Psychiatric Association,* revised May 2000, 1.

66. Ibid., 4.

67. Ibid., 2.

gay men and lesbians. Studies of judgment, stability, reliability, and social and vocational adaptiveness all show that gay men and lesbians function every bit as well as heterosexuals. Nor is homosexuality a matter of individual choice. Research suggests that the homosexual orientation is in place very early in the life cycle, possibly even before birth. It is found in about ten percent of the population, a figure that is surprisingly constant across cultures, irrespective of the different moral values and standards of a particular culture. Contrary to what some imply, the incidence of homosexuality in a population does not appear to change with new moral codes or social mores. Research findings suggest that efforts to repair homosexuals are nothing more than social prejudice garbed in psychological accouterments.[68]

A number of individuals who consider themselves Christians and are also in the science or medicine areas have written articles, given presentations, and otherwise expressed their views on the issue of homosexuality. Many of those people who have taken the most strident and most negative position on the issue are from the religious right. For example, Jeffrey B. Satinover, a psychiatrist, has spoken for the Family Research Council in 1996 at a Capitol Hill briefing regarding the Defense of Marriage Act. Dr. Satinover, in his critique on the hearings, unfortunately shows a lack of understanding for how science works. He criticizes many of the presentations concerning a genetic link for homosexuality by stating that their research did not *prove* (emphasis mine) such a link. He is right — science cannot prove anything, but can only disprove. He has many other misconceptions as well; for example, in attempting to explain the difference between *heritable* and *inherited,* he states that "inherited" means "determined directly by genes," which is wrong. An inherited trait, if expressed, is determined by environment; the genes for the trait simply set the limits of expression.

---

68. J. J. Conger, "Proceedings of the American Psychological Association, Incorporated, for the Year 1974: Minutes of the Annual Meeting of the Council of Representatives," *American Psychologist* 30 (1975): 620–51.

The many misconceptions that Dr. Satinover expresses are not unusual, and many highly educated and intelligent individuals have such misconceptions about how science works and how it can or cannot be used. In his conclusions, Dr. Satinover brings forward what he considers to be the two major ideas concerning homosexuality: that it is (1) "genetic" and (2) unchangeable. He dogmatically declares that neither statement is true, and that in fact substantial scientific evidence exists to the contrary. If we think of "truth" as absolute, of course Dr. Satinover is correct. But scientists do not think that way. As discussed earlier in this unit, to the biologist truth is probabilistic. Much debate continues concerning the biological aspects of homosexuality. Much of the evidence has questionable methodology, logic, or is otherwise flawed. However, a great deal of evidence is still available that while science cannot "prove" a genetic link to homosexuality, nonetheless such a link is strongly suggested. Much of the work that attempts to disprove a link between homosexuality and genetics is likewise flawed. If we were to place the two opposing sets of data on a scale, the "substantial scientific evidence" cited by Satinover would not outweigh that supporting a genetic link. In regard to his second statement, whether homosexual behavior can be changed to heterosexual behavior, his own professional organization has provided a vast amount of evidence that indicates the danger and futility of such an attempt, but that story is not significant to our present discussion.[69]

As the businessperson might say, what is the bottom line? Might one draw any conclusions about the biological basis for the human condition of homosexuality? To that question the scientist would give a guarded yes. While neither overwhelming nor conclusive, that evidence strongly suggests a biological basis for homosexuality while at the same time recognizing an environmental and social influence. (However, no evidence for a "homosexual gene" presently exists.) To the Christian the impli-

---

69. J. B. Satinover, "Statement on Homosexuality: A Speech Presented at a July 2, 1996, Capitol Hill Briefing regarding the Defense of Marriage Act," presented in *At the Podium,* a publication of the Family Research Council, Washington, D.C. *www.frc.org/podium/pd96g4hs.html,* 14.

cation is that we should not judge homosexuals: judgment in any case is for God. Nor should we assume that an individual adopts a homosexual lifestyle as the result of a rational, informed choice. We certainly should not assume that homosexuals are marred in some way or incapable of trust or leadership. Neither should we assume that they would rather be heterosexual and thus try to mold them to our personal standard of human sexual behavior. They, as we, are children of God and should be accorded the love and consideration that Christ has instructed us to show for one another, and which is, in fact, a requirement of our Christian faith. The role of the homosexual, as well as the heterosexual, within the Church should be based upon common criteria for all; love of Christ, belief in God, and consideration of the special gifts, talents, experiences, and dedication that an individual can bring to the Church.

WHEN SCIENCE DIVERGES FROM SCRIPTURE

Having considered what biologists say about the physical basis of sexual orientation and behavior, which appears to conflict with the biblical stance, we now turn to history to look at the ways Christians have dealt with conflicts between science and scripture in the past. Since fairly early in church history, many thoughtful Christians have striven to reconcile the truth of the Bible with science. The most important episodes in this struggle were the flat earth versus round earth controversy, the geocentric (earth-centered) versus heliocentric (sun-centered) cosmos conflict, and the theory of evolution versus what is now called creationism. In this chapter we examine the history of these controversies to discern what principles the Christian community has developed about how interpreters should deal with apparent or real conflicts between science and the Bible.

First, a brief overview. Contrary to the popular belief that religion and science are locked in mortal combat, Christian biblical interpreters have responded to scientific advances in a variety of ways, sometimes positively and sometimes negatively. The combat "mythology" was created in part by two influential books written at the end of the nineteenth century, one British and one American: J. W. Draper's *History of the Conflict between Religion and Science* (1875) and A. D. White's *A History of the Warfare of Science with Theology in Christendom* (1896). Modern historians, who realize that history is more complex than the combat model suggests, no longer take these books seriously. Nevertheless, they reflect the mood created by the battles over evolution, which in some quarters continue to this day.

The first and least well known of the episodes we will consider is the debate over whether the earth is flat or spherical. Since the earth's roundness is taken for granted today, some readers may be surprised that this controversy spanned many centuries and that the Bible reflects the view that the earth is flat. The church fathers also pondered other similar problems such as the composition of the heavens, but the question of the shape of the earth is representative of their thinking on natural science.

The second episode occurred during the sixteenth and seventeenth centuries when both Roman Catholic and Protestant churches were faced with how to respond to Copernicus's heliocentric (sun-centered) views when biblical texts were written from a geocentric (earth-centered) perspective. Although many people know the story of Galileo's trial and conviction for his Copernican views and his recantation, a careful look at the record reveals that religion was not the only factor that led to his conviction. A perusal of Protestant responses also leads to some interesting surprises for people who assume that the churches' reaction to scientific advances was always negative.

Finally, the evolutionary theory of Charles Darwin in the nineteenth century challenged a literal reading of the stories of the creation of humanity in Genesis. New discoveries in the field of geology that conflicted with the biblical view of the age of the earth paved the way for Darwin's even more difficult material. Here again, the record is not as simple and straightforward as one might suspect.

The Shape of the Earth

Even before the birth of Christ, Greek philosophers (the word "scientist" developed later) had already concluded that the earth was spherical rather than flat. This determination came not as a result of direct observation, but based on their philosophical belief that the most natural shape is the sphere. For example, a falling drop of water turns into a spherical shape.

The earliest Christian writers displayed no hostility toward the scientific work of their day. For example, the early Christian writer

Clement of Rome in his letter to the Corinthians (c. 96 C.E.) mentions the Antipodes, the name given by those who believed the earth was round to people who were thought to dwell on the opposite side of the earth. Clement of Rome in no way criticizes this view. Clement of Alexandria (c. 200 C.E.), using the allegorical method of interpretation popular in his city, understood the Tabernacle (the tent in which the Israelites worshiped before the construction of the Temple) and its furnishings to represent the world. In particular he believed the six winged golden cherubim stood for either the two Bears (constellations), or more likely the two hemispheres of the earth (*Miscellanies*). The latter possibility of course was dependent on his acceptance of the roundness of the earth.

Jerome (c. 345–c. 420), the translator of the Vulgate (the Latin Bible), would later challenge Clement's views. Jerome opposed those who followed "the stupid wisdom of the philosophers" and who believed the cherubim in the tabernacle were the two hemispheres, the one on which they lived and the other, the Antipodes (the lower half; *Commentary on Ezekiel,* chaps. 1 and 5). The views of Basil were moderate. He wrote a treatise on the six days of creation (c. 360) suggesting that humans do not need to know whether the earth is flat or round and other similar matters. He neither denied nor affirmed secular science, yet he did try to show the possibility of accepting the results of scientific investigation without danger to the faith. Ambrose (d. 397), whose views are similar to Basil's in that he did not think humans needed to know about the earth's shape, nevertheless often referred to it as a sphere (*The Six Days of Creation;* I, 3, ¶9; VI, 2, ¶7).

The first and most adamant of the people who opposed the roundness of the earth was Lactantius, whose *Divine Institutions* in seven volumes were written between 302 and 323. The twenty-fourth chapter of the third book, *On the False Wisdom of the Philosophers,* ridiculed the idea of the earth's sphericity as well as the notion of Antipodes. In the sixth century, Cosmas Indicopleustes, a merchant who became a monk, insisted on the literal interpretation of the scriptures. Based on an extremely literal reading of Isaiah 40:22, "It is he [God] who sits above the circle of the earth . . . ," he defended the flatness of the earth.[1] In the long run the views of Augustine (354–430) had the biggest impact. His view of science was relatively positive. He was not hostile to Greek science, though he also took scripture very seriously.[2] He wrote:

> One does not read in the Gospel that the Lord said: I will send to you the Paraclete who will teach you about the course of the sun and moon. For He willed to make them Christians, not mathematicians. (*De actis cum Felice Manichaeo*, I, 10)

On another occasion he said:

> It is also frequently asked what our belief must be about the form and shape of heaven according to Sacred Scripture. Many scholars engage in lengthy discussions on these matters, but the sacred writers with their deeper wisdom have omitted them. . . . Hence, I must say briefly that in the matter of the shape of heaven the sacred writers knew the truth, but that the Spirit of God, who spoke through them, did not wish to teach men these facts that would be of no avail for their salvation. (*The Literal Meaning of Genesis*)

Nevertheless, Augustine also taught that biblical language was authoritative unless clearly demonstrated proofs of physical truth were available to contravene.[3]

For this reason Augustine rejected the idea that people might inhabit the opposite side of the world because no evidence existed for it. He suggested that even if the earth were a sphere, no reason necessarily was available to believe that humans lived on the other side (*The City of God* XVI, 9).

---

1. John Dillenberger, *Protestant Thought and Natural Science: Historical Interpretation* (Garden City, N.Y.: Doubleday, 1960), 21.

2. J. L. E. Dreyer, *A History of Astronomy from Thales to Kepler* (New York: Dover Publications, 1953), 213–14.

3. Kenneth J. Howell, "Galileo and the History of Hermeneutics," in *Facets of Faith and Science,* vol. 4: *Interpreting God's Action in the World,* ed. Jitsu M. Van der Meer (Lanham, Md.: University Press of America, 1997), 252.

A statement Augustine made in the *Enchiridion* that sounds very negative about science is often quoted:

> When it is asked what we ought to believe in matters of religion, the answer is not to be sought in the exploration of the nature of things, after the manner of those whom the Greeks called "physicists." Nor should we be dismayed if Christians are ignorant about the properties and the number of the basic elements of nature, or about the motion, order, and deviations of the stars, the map of the heavens, the kinds and nature of animals, plants, stones, springs, rivers, and mountains; about the divisions of space and time, about the signs of impending storms, and the myriad other things which these "physicists" have come to understand, or think they have.... [F]or the Christian, it is enough to believe that the cause of all created things, whether in heaven or on earth, whether visible or invisible, is nothing other than the goodness of the Creator, who is the one and the true God. (*Enchiridion,* 3, ¶9)

What should be emphasized is Augustine's opening words, "what we ought to believe *in matters of religion.*" In other words what Augustine was saying was that from a theological point of view what matters is that we acknowledge the goodness of creation. When scientific knowledge was needed, Augustine believed that the Bible was not the place to seek it. He wrote:

> Usually, even a non-Christian knows something about the earth, the heavens, and the other elements of this world, about the motion and orbit of the stars and even their size and relative positions, about the predictable eclipses of the sun and moon, the cycles of the years and the seasons, about the kinds of animals, shrubs, stones, and so forth, and this knowledge he holds to as being certain from reason and experience. Now it is a disgraceful and dangerous thing for an infidel to hear a Christian, presumably giving the meaning of Holy Scripture, talking nonsense on these topics; and we should take all means to present such an embarrassing situ-

ation, in which people show up vast ignorance in a Christian and laugh it to scorn. (*The Literal Meaning of Genesis,* I, 19, ¶39)

The next important voice was that of Isidore, Bishop of Seville (c. 570–636), whose *Etymologies* includes references to the Greek views on the roundness of the earth and the existence of Antipodes without repudiating these ideas. The Venerable Bede (b. c. 673) was also a moderate. In his *De natura rerum* he states the views of Pliny, almost verbatim at times, including the sphericity of the earth. By the eighth century, the conviction that secular and biblical learning were antithetical was on the wane, and many educated church leaders recognized that the earth was round.[4]

By the ninth century the roundness of the earth was generally accepted, as the Greek philosophers had accepted it from the time of Plato. Theologians had not changed their understanding of what the biblical authors meant. Rather the scientific evidence was too strong to be rejected; for the sake of its authority, the Bible had to be shown to be in conformity with scientific evidence.[5]

The Copernican Revolution

Until recently little scholarly work had been done on the methods of biblical interpretation used to understand biblical passages whose traditional interpretations were in conflict with the emerging science of the sixteenth and seventeenth centuries. This lack is surprising because a great deal of attention was paid at the time to how to reconcile the new discoveries with the Bible. The most common metaphor for envisioning the relationship between science and religion was God's two books. The book of nature was thought to be God's handiwork and a proper object of human investigation, the results of which would glorify God. Many scientists believed that the study of nature was a religious duty analogous to the careful study of the Bible. In addition, virtually

---

4. Dreyer, *A History of Astronomy,* 219–25.
5. Paul H. Kocher, *Science and Religion in Elizabethan England* (New York: Octagon Books, 1969), 190.

everyone accepted the Bible as true. Almost no one questioned its authority. When advocates of the new science developed their arguments, they did not deny the validity of scripture or its authority. They believed that the two books could not contradict each other.[6]

In the centuries before Nicholas Copernicus (1473–1543), the accepted view of the universe was geocentric. This view was based on a combination of the physics of Aristotle (378–322 B.C.E.) and the astronomy of Ptolemy (fl. 150 B.C.E.). These views became available to the West by way of the Arabs in the twelfth century. John of Holywood (d. 1256), known as Sacrobosco, recorded a combination of the two systems. This eclectic picture of the universe in which the earth was at the center, but somewhat off-center to account for certain movements of the planets, and in which the planets moved through a complicated set of epicycles (complex gyrating orbits) enjoyed wide acceptance.[7]

Copernicus was born in Poland, orphaned at ten years old, and adopted by his uncle, who was a Catholic priest and who sent young Nicholas to the University of Cracow for a course of general studies. Afterwards Copernicus went to the University of Bologna to study canon law, but he also had time for courses in mathematics and astronomy. While at Bologna, Copernicus became convinced that the reigning astronomical model was too complex to be right. He searched through the history of thought for a better model, and he found that some ancient thinkers believed that the earth was not at rest, but in fact moved.

Copernicus continued his education at the University of Padua where he studied medicine and law. In 1506 he became personal physician to his aging uncle. During the six years he spent in this occupation, he had time to study astronomy. After his uncle's death, Copernicus took up a post that his uncle had secured for him as canon of the Frauenburg Cathedral. There Copernicus

---

6. Kenneth J. Howell, "Copernicanism and the Bible in Early Modern Science," in *Facets of Faith and Science,* ed. Van der Meer, 262–63.

7. Jerome J. Langford, *Galileo, Science and the Church* (Ann Arbor: University of Michigan, 1971), 23–32.

set up an observatory; when he was not busy with his canonical duties, he could work on his astronomical studies.

In 1530 Copernicus circulated among his friends an outline of his astronomy. The outline attracted much attention, including that of Pope Clement VII who was favorably impressed. Urged to publish the outline, Copernicus did not want to for fear of ridicule. Although the ridicule he feared was probably primarily scientific, theological elements were also included. Copernicus was aware that his views seemed to be at odds with scriptural teachings. In the dedication of his book to Pope Paul III he alluded to the follies of Lactantius (the founder of the church who had most vehemently held that the scriptures were authoritative in matters of science) and contended that his system did not contradict scripture, though he did not explain how he reconciled the two.[8] His work was not suspended by the Catholic Church until 1616, years after his death.

In Copernicus's system, the sun rather than the earth is at the center of the universe and the earth is just one of many planets that revolve around the sun. Copernicus assumed that the planetary orbits were circular (they are actually elliptical) and as a result still had to resort to the same eccentrics and epicycles that the Ptolemaic system used. Thus, Copernicus's system, though on the right track, was still complicated and was not the obvious improvement that in retrospect we think it was.[9]

Copernicanism among the Protestants

In 1539 Martin Luther is reported to have said:

> People give ear to an upstart astrologer who strove to show that the earth revolves, not the heavens or the firmament, the sun and the moon. Whosoever wishes to appear clever must devise some new system which of all systems, of course, is the very best. This fool wishes to reverse the entire science of astronomy; but Sacred Scripture tells us that

---

8. Kocher, *Science and Religion*, 190.
9. Langford, *Galileo, Science and the Church*, 37.

Josue [Joshua] commanded the sun to stand still, and not the earth.[10]

Whether Luther actually said this is not clear, but if he did the remark was an off-hand one pronounced at a time when Copernicus's views were only known through hearsay.[11]

A close associate of Martin Luther (1483–1546), the Protestant reformer Philipp Melanchthon (1497–1560), made many reforms in the German universities. He believed that mathematics and astronomy deserved to be in the curriculum. As a result, a strong tradition of mathematical astronomy developed at Wittenberg.[12] A professor there named Georg Joachim Rheticus (1514–76) went to visit Copernicus to learn of his system. The result was Rheticus's *Narratio Prima,* a brief description of Copernicus's system, published in 1540. During the following years, the new hypothesis evoked much discussion, both about astronomy as a discipline and the theological acceptability of the notion of the earth's mobility.[13]

A Lutheran pastor of Nuremberg, Andreas Osiander (1498–1552), trying to deal with both the acceptability of astronomy as a discipline and the theological acceptability of Copernicanism, wrote an unsigned preface for Copernicus's book *De revolutionibus orbium coelestium.* This book was not published until 1543. Copernicus received an advance copy just hours before his death. Osiander's perspective was that the astronomer's job was to account for the celestial appearances, not to determine the actual nature of the universe. While Copernicus intended his system as an actual account of the universe, Osiander was concerned to fend off criticism with his (then) conventional approach to astronomy. Theology and physics, not astronomy, were thought to be sources of actual truth. Rheticus, like Copernicus, understood Copernicus's system to describe actual physical reality. Thus Rheticus

---

10. Ibid., 35.
11. Dillenberger, *Protestant Thought and Natural Science,* 37–38.
12. Robert S. Westman, "The Copernicans and the Churches," in *God and Nature: Historical Essays on the Encounter between Christianity and Science,* ed. David C. Lindberg and Ronald L. Numbers (Berkeley: University of California, 1986), 82.
13. Howell, "Copernicanism and the Bible," 264.

attempted in his book to deal with the conflict between Copernicanism and the Bible. He relied on earlier traditions, arguing that
the Bible's purpose was not to present natural philosophy (i.e.,
science), but rather to lead to salvation.[14]
Rheticus's positive attitude toward Copernicus's work was not
universal in Wittenberg. Philipp Melanchthon argued against the
heliocentric approach using three arguments. He claimed that it
was contrary to Aristotelian physics, astronomical observations,
and scripture. He wrote:

> The eyes are witnesses that the heavens revolve in the space
> of twenty-four hours. But certain men, either from the love
> of novelty, or to make a display of ingenuity, have concluded
> that the earth moves.... Now it is a want of honesty and
> decency to assert such notions publicly, and the example is
> pernicious. (*First Doctrines of Physics*)

Melanchthon's opposition was not based so much on scriptural
objections as on philosophical ones. He believed that Copernicus was reviving erroneous ideas that had long since been
discredited.[15] He did not oppose Copernicus's system as a mathematical hypothesis, only as a description of actual reality. Since
Melanchthon believed that astronomy was, by definition, unable
to give a true picture of physical reality, the Bible could be used
to settle the issue. He cited Psalm 93 which says that God has
established the world and it will never be moved. If the earth is
immobile, then it cannot revolve around the sun (Ps. 93:1).[16]
Although Melanchthon opposed Copernicanism, he did not
forbid its inclusion in the curriculum. On the contrary, due to
his influence on the German universities, astronomy in general
and Copernicanism in particular were widely taught and studied
in northern Europe. One influential teacher was the astronomer
of Tübingen, Michael Mastlin. He was also a Lutheran pastor.
During a forty-seven-year tenure, he regularly introduced his
students to Copernican views. One of his students was Johann

14. Ibid.
15. Dillenberger, *Protestant Thought and Natural Science*, 39–41.
16. Howell, "Copernicanism and the Bible," 264–65.

Kepler (1571–1630), who developed some of the new physics that complemented Copernicus's new astronomy.[17]

Kepler was concerned with the biblical interpretive issues surrounding the Copernican theory. Like many before him, he believed that the Bible does not intend to teach science, but rather accommodates its language to the common people.

> Astronomy attempts to understand the causes which are operative in nature and to correct illusions of sight. The holy writings, which teach us of more sublime things, use the habitual language of men to be understood and in the cases where it speaks of natural things . . . they do so according to the appearances which are evident to sight and which serve as the basis of human language. The Scriptures would not be expressed in any other way, when all men know perfectly all the illusions of sight. . . . We should not require of the Scriptures on this point that it abandon ordinary language to adopt that of science, to speak in abstract and difficult terms which exceed the understanding of those it wishes to instruct. If such were the case, it would trouble simple believers and block the way to the true goal which it has and which is more sublime. (*The Epitome of Copernican Astronomy*)

Scholars have long debated whether the Genevan reformer John Calvin (1509–64) opposed Copernicanism. The consensus now is that he probably was not aware of Copernican ideas and thus did not oppose them. Nevertheless, the way Calvin handled other matters relating to physical phenomena influenced later Protestant interpreters. He often invoked the principle of accommodation. He understood the purpose of scripture to be instruction in salvation, not cosmology. At times, he seemed anxious to protect the Bible from criticism that it had an inferior cosmology. He said that scripture is designed to teach ordinary people. Astronomy and other similar knowledge must be learned elsewhere.[18] He wrote:

---

17. Ibid., 265–66.
18. Ibid., 268.

The Holy Spirit had no intention to teach astronomy; and in proposing instruction meant to be common to the simplest and most uneducated persons, he made use by Moses and the other prophets of popular language, that none might shelter himself under the pretext of obscurity, as we will see men sometimes very readily pretend an incapacity to understand, when anything deep and recondite is submitted to their notice. Accordingly... the Holy Spirit would rather speak childishly than unintelligibly to the humble and unlearned. (*Commentary on the Psalms*, vol. 5)

Calvin probably influenced a number of Protestant thinkers of the sixteenth and seventeenth centuries, all advocates of Copernicanism, including Francis Bacon (1561–1626) and John Wilkins (1614–72) in England and Simon Stevin (1548–1620) and Andre Rivet (1573–1651) in the Netherlands. Perhaps Calvin's influence on the New England Puritans also created the climate in which Copernicanism never caused much stir. As it became evident that the earth indeed revolves around the sun, the Puritan theologians accepted this new astronomy without the contention it caused elsewhere.[19]

Several Reformed theologians in Holland opposed Copernicus's views on scriptural grounds. The best-known among them is Gisbertus Voetius (1589–1676), a professor of theology at Utrecht.[20] In the latter part of the sixteenth century in continental Europe, a kind of Protestant scholasticism developed in which scripture was seen as a repository of metaphysical knowledge. Its inerrancy was also emphasized. This development led to more serious Protestant opposition to Copernican views than had been true during the Reformation.[21]

The theological criticism of Copernicanism was milder in England than on the European continent. Opponents and proponents both tended to be church leaders. Proponents relied on the

---

19. Perry Miller, *The New England Mind: The Seventeenth Century* (Boston: Beacon Press, 1961), 217.
20. "Copernicanism and the Bible," 269–71.
21. Dillenberger, *Protestant Thought and Natural Science*, 50–73.

argument that God had accommodated the scriptures to the limitations of human minds. Opponents were uncomfortable with this approach, but had to admit that with respect to biblical passages describing windows in the sky and four corners on the earth, some such approach was necessary. The debate was not simply a theological one, however. As was true elsewhere, scientific questions combined with theological ones to prevent Copernicus's heliocentric system from gaining immediate unanimous acceptance. As the evidence mounted over the years, especially with Isaac Newton's work, the controversies melted away and Copernicus's views became the norm.[22]

Galileo and the Roman Catholic Church

In Catholic Europe where the church councils were considered infallible, the Council of Trent (1545–63) provided the framework for biblical interpretation. This Council forbade private interpretation of the Bible, reserving this right and responsibility to the Church, and prohibited publishing or even holding opinions contrary to the unanimous witness of the founders of the church. In addition, the Protestant Reformation — with its understanding of the sacraments, penance, and the papacy — led to an emphasis on literal interpretation.[23]

Galileo (1564–1642) was the best-known among Roman Catholics who championed Copernicus's work, though he was not alone. Galileo was born in Pisa, Italy. At the age of seventeen, after receiving his basic education at a monastery near Florence, he entered the University of Pisa, where he studied for a liberal arts degree. His father had planned for him to study medicine, but after four years of study the money ran out, so Galileo left without a degree. Nevertheless, he continued to study on his own. At the age of twenty-two he invented a hydrostatic balance and two years later his work on the center of gravity in solids re-

22. Kocher, *Science and Religion,* 197–200.
23. Howell, "Copernicanism and the Bible," 271–72.

ceived critical acclaim. One person whom Galileo impressed was a mathematician who was able to obtain a post for him as professor of mathematics at the University of Pisa, the same university where Galileo had studied but never received his degree.[24] The next two years were difficult for Galileo. He was increasingly dissatisfied with Aristotle's views. The story goes that he dropped two objects of different weights from the Leaning Tower of Pisa. They landed at the same time, thus disproving Aristotle's belief that heavier bodies fall faster than lighter ones. Whether apocryphal or true, the story exemplifies Galileo's spirit of direct observation and thoughtful argument. Galileo's colleagues were not pleased when this young professor who did not even have a degree dared to challenge Aristotle. Not only did Galileo reject accepted views; he often coupled his unconventional beliefs with sarcastic attacks on his opponents. The tension was so high that in 1591 Galileo resigned his post.[25]

The same mathematician who had obtained the professorship for him at Pisa then recommended him for a position at the University of Padua in the republic of Venice. Here the atmosphere was more relaxed, his salary was higher, and he lived with a woman, Marina Gamba, who bore him a son and two daughters, though they never married. Here he also became deeply interested in astronomy.[26] When Galileo first came to Padua in 1592 he was probably still teaching the Ptolemaic geocentric system, but by 1594 he had accepted Copernicus's heliocentric system. Proving this hypothesis became the burning passion of his life. In 1608 the first telescope was made. Within a year Galileo was making one for himself. He made two more, each better than the last. With the third one, he made many discoveries. He saw that the moon was not the smooth sphere it had been supposed to be, but in fact had valleys and hills just like the earth. He discovered that Jupiter had moons of its own.[27]

---

24. Langford, *Galileo, Science and the Church*, 18–19.
25. Ibid., 19–22.
26. Ibid., 22.
27. Ibid., 39.

In 1610 Galileo moved back to the University of Pisa with an honorary chair in mathematics. With no teaching obligations, he could pursue his studies full-time. All was not well, however. Many of the professors at Pisa were reluctant to accept Galileo's views. They contradicted too much of the accepted physics of the day. Without a new physics to supplement the new astronomy, many questions remained unanswered.[28]

In 1609 the German Johann Kepler had published his *Astronomica nova,* in which he showed that the planetary orbits were elliptical rather than circular. If Galileo had incorporated Kepler's work into the Copernican theory, a simpler and more accurate system would have resulted. Unfortunately, Kepler was also interested in astrology. The speculative superstitious elements in his works probably kept Galileo from taking him seriously.[29]

Although the initial objections to Galileo's support of the Copernican theory were scientific, scriptural objections also surfaced. In 1612 Lodovico delle Colombe was the first to cite scripture directly against Galileo, although he did not mention Galileo's name. In 1613 Galileo published his *Letters on the Sunspots,* the first time he had come out in print to support Copernicus. He published this work in Italian rather than Latin, making it widely accessible.

The controversy then became more widespread. People wanted to know why Joshua would have commanded the sun to stand still if in fact it did not move (Josh. 10:12–13). They wondered how to deal with Psalm 93:1, which says,

> The Lord is king, he is robed in majesty;
>   the Lord is robed, he is girded with strength.
> He has established the world; it shall never be moved.

or with Psalm 104:5, which reads:

> You set the earth on its foundations,
>   so that it shall never be shaken.

---

28. Ibid., 40–44.
29. Ibid., 44–49.

or with Psalm 19:4b–6, which declares:

> In the heavens he has set a tent for the sun,
> which comes out like a bridegroom from his wedding
>   canopy,
> and like a strong man runs its course with joy.
> Its rising is from the end of the heavens,
>   and its circuit to the end of them;
> and nothing is hid from its heat.[30]

In 1615 Galileo decided to respond to these questions in a long letter to Benedetto Castelli, a friend, supporter, and the chief mathematician at the University of Pisa. The occasion of the letter was a dinner in which Castelli had responded to the Grand Duchess Christina's questions and then sent Galileo an account of what had happened, to which Galileo had replied.[31] Although Galileo's purpose was to silence theological objections to Copernicus, his effort turned out to be counterproductive. From a Catholic perspective it was one thing for a scientist to be a scientist; it was quite another for him to dabble in theology.[32]

A copy of Galileo's letter was sent to the Inquisitors General in Rome. When Galileo heard about it, he sent his own copy to make sure they at least had an accurate version of the letter. He also sent a note explaining that the letter had been written hastily and that he was revising it. In this letter, now called a *Letter to the Grand Duchess Christina,* Galileo was not trying to show that the Copernican theory was taught in the Bible. Rather, he was attempting to remove scriptural objections to it. He believed that to try to prove any physical theory from the Bible was fruitless and would wreak havoc on the church. So Galileo's first point was that the Bible's purpose is to show the way to salvation, not to teach physical science.[33]

Galileo's second point was that if demonstrable scientific evidence of a physical theory was available, the Bible had to be

30. Ibid., 50–53.
31. Ibid., 57–58.
32. Ibid., 53–55.
33. Howell, "Copernicanism and the Bible," 246–47.

interpreted in light of it. He was convinced that the Bible never contradicts physical reality. He also believed that he had demonstrable evidence of Copernicanism.[34] Others at this time were not so sure.[35]

Galileo's third point was that the Copernican system was more consistent with scripture than the old Ptolemaic one. He supported this point by suggesting that the sun rotates on its axis and through this motion exerts an influence on the planets to move around it. Thus, if the sun stopped rotating, the planets would stop their motion and that day would be lengthened. Then Joshua's words about the sun standing still could be understood literally. This interpretation seems odd in light of Galileo's first point that scripture does not intend to teach science.[36]

Of all the solutions to this oddity that scholars offer, Kenneth Howell's is most plausible. He argues that given the emphasis in the Council of Trent on the witness of the founders of the church, Galileo structured his argument along Augustinian lines. He suggests that Galileo was structuring his tripartite argument on Augustine's treatment of similar problems. In considering the shape of the heavens, Augustine advocated distinguishing questions of physical science from questions of faith. He used the principle of accommodation to explain the biblical descriptions. In other words, God used language and conceptions of physical reality that were accessible to the people with whom God was trying to communicate. Galileo's first point was along these lines.[37]

Augustine went on, however, to lay down another principle: that the words of scripture must be accepted if uncertainty persists about a physical question. However, if demonstrable proofs existed, then the interpreter had to take these into account when interpreting the Bible. This approach constituted Galileo's second point.[38]

Augustine also resorted to unusual literal interpretations. Re-

34. Howell, "Galileo and the History of Hermeneutics," 247–49.
35. Langford, *Galileo, Science and the Church,* 68.
36. Howell, "Galileo and the History of Hermeneutics," 249.
37. Ibid., 250–51.
38. Ibid., 252.

sponding to an imaginary questioner who was concerned about the biblical description of heaven as a vault — which contradicted commentators who thought heaven was a sphere — he responded that a literal interpretation did not contradict the sphericity of the heavens, if one keeps in mind the limited position of an earthly observer![39] Galileo's third point involved a similarly strained interpretation.

Galileo preferred the first argument: science and theology are distinct. The second position, that the words of scripture were authoritative unless demonstrable physical proof existed of a conflicting theory, was a fallback position. His third position was his response if pushed against a wall. He probably did not really believe that the Bible taught the Copernican system, but he could interpret the Bible in such a way as to suggest this belief if pressed hard enough.[40]

The revised version of Galileo's letter was not sent until after another important episode. A Carmelite friar, Paolo Antonio Foscarini (1373–1457), wrote a letter that tried to reconcile the Copernican system with scripture. He argued that the Bible was designed to foster salvation and was not a scientific treatise. He also argued that scripture must be reconciled with science when the results of science were certainly correct. Perhaps bolstered by this work of a theologian, Galileo wrote to his friend the Archbishop of Rome, Piero Dini, saying he wanted Copernicus's system accepted as a fact or rejected completely. He could not settle for a compromise.[41]

The response of Cardinal Bellarmine (1542–1621) to Foscarini's book urged that Foscarini and (indirectly) Galileo view Copernicus's system as a hypothesis only. Bellarmine went on to quote the Council of Trent, which forbade going against the teaching of the founders of the church when it was unanimous and when the subject matter was one that was a matter of faith or morals. The majority of church founders certainly believed in a geocentric universe, but they did not unanimously agree that the question

39. Ibid.
40. Ibid., 252–53.
41. Langford, *Galileo, Science and the Church,* 59.

was a matter of faith or morals.[42] Augustine, for one, did not believe that the question raised was one of faith or morality (*The Literal Meaning of Genesis* II, 9, ¶20).

Bellarmine introduced a new distinction, however, speaking of matters of faith "by reason of subject matter" and those "by reason of the one who speaks." Thus he argued that even though the earth's lack of motion is not a matter of faith in terms of its subject matter, the question is a matter of faith in terms of authorship because the Holy Spirit made the point in various scriptures. Ultimately, his argument was that the traditional exegesis of the relevant scriptural passages should stand until proof of Copernicus's hypothesis emerged.

Nevertheless, in 1616 the Holy Office of Rome cleared Galileo's name. Galileo was not satisfied. He was still eager to have Copernicus's system accepted. Claiming new proof, and working through Cardinal Orsini, he approached Pope Paul V, who summoned his theological consulters to give a formal decision. They censured the notions of the sun's immobility and of the earth's mobility, the first as being directly contrary to scripture and the second as being indirectly contrary.[43]

The following month Copernicus's *De revolutionibus* was suspended until corrected and Foscarini's book was condemned outright. The preface to Copernicus's work, though it was not written by Copernicus, but by Osiander, and included without Copernicus's knowledge, indicated that the astronomical system was hypothetical rather than real, but Foscarini's book attempted to prove that the Copernican system as a reality did not contradict scripture, which was another matter altogether. Galileo was disappointed but not defeated. He knew that the decision might still possibly be reversed. He returned home and went back to work.[44]

In 1618 Francesco Ingoli published a book in which he argued against the Copernican system on three grounds in descending order: mathematical problems, problems with the physics of Copernicanism, and theological problems. His view was that

42. Ibid., 60–63.
43. Ibid., 87–90.
44. Ibid., 97–105.

the literal meaning of scripture should be followed unless compelling evidence for reinterpretation was available, which he did not believe existed at that time.[45]

In 1622 Tommaso Campanella (1568–1639), a Dominican friar, published an extensive defense of the Copernican system. Like other defenses, he argued for a distinction between matters of faith and science, a distinction he found in both Augustine and Aquinas. He also argued that in some respects a literal reading of the Bible was more consistent with the new science than the old science.[46] The reason that this book was not placed on the index of prohibited works is not clear.

In 1632 Galileo created a major crisis with his publication of *Dialogue on the Great World Systems.* Although the preface promised an impartial discussion, many readers felt that the book obviously was a veiled defense of the Copernican system. This approach was forbidden because the notions of the mobility of the earth and immobility of the sun had been censured in 1616. Galileo proceeded to publish his work because the political climate seemed good and indeed he was able to obtain the Roman imprimatur for his book, but his enemies were ready to pounce on him. They took advantage of the opportunity.[47]

Galileo was summoned to Rome to be tried. The result was that his book was prohibited and he was required to make a formal disavowal of his heretical opinions. Not until 1822, almost two hundred years later, were Copernican writings taken off the index of prohibited works.[48]

The New Geology

Ironically, at the time when the controversies surrounding Copernican views finally died down, new issues were on the scene. Discoveries in geology laid some of the groundwork for the work

---

45. Howell, "Copernicanism and the Bible," 272–73.
46. Ibid., 276–77.
47. Langford, *Galileo, Science and the Church,* 105–36.
48. Ibid.,137–58.

of Charles Darwin but also prompted new debates. The new geology suggested that the earth was vastly older than anyone had previously thought. If this timeline were accurate, then the thousands of years needed for the various species to develop according to Darwin's theory had in fact elapsed.

At the end of the eighteenth and beginning of the nineteenth centuries, the study of the earth's crust — with its layers and fossil deposits — raised about the age of the earth difficult questions that seemed to contradict biblical chronology. The many thousands of years that scientists believed it had taken for the earth to form called into question the famous calculation of the scholarly seventeenth-century Irish archbishop Ussher (1580–1656) that God created the world in 4004 B.C.E., a calculation that was not original with him.[49] Although some thinking Christians had already abandoned a literal interpretation of Genesis, for others the new scientific views were extremely unsettling.[50]

Two views, named after Neptune and Vulcan, predominated among geologists. The former suggested that the earth had once been covered by the sea and the rocks now in the earth's crust were formed by the movement of the water. The Vulcanists argued that the rocks were a result of the earth's internal heat, not the action of water. The Vulcan view eventually held sway. The chief proponent of the Vulcan view, James Hutton (1726–97), believed that the key to understanding the geological history of the earth was processes that were currently observable. In addition he proposed that the orderly and uniform geological forces had taken a very long time to shape the earth into its present form. Hutton's view was called "uniformitarianism," as opposed to an alternative view known as "catastrophism," in which a series of catastrophic geological events were assumed to have shaped the earth. Noah's flood fit nicely into this latter view.

---

49. Martin J. S. Rudwick, "The Shape and Meaning of Earth History," in *God and Nature,* ed. Lindberg and Numbers, 296.

50. D. F. Bratchell, *The Impact of Darwinism: Texts and Commentary Illustrating Nineteenth-Century Religious, Scientific and Literary Attitudes* (Amersham, Buckinghamshire, U.K.: Avebury, 1981), 16.

Charles Lyell (1797–1875), professor of geology at King's College in London from 1831 to 1833, developed uniformitarianism into a serious scientific theory. Lyell's three-volume *Principles of Geology* became the standard work of his time and through the mid-nineteenth century. His understanding of a vastly large time frame for the development of the earth and of slow development caused by regular natural processes was an important underpinning for Darwin's work. Geologists differed in their acceptance of the new theories and their understanding of Genesis in light of these theories.[51] Biblical interpreters reacted in various ways, but rarely did they continue to subscribe to a literal recent six-day creation.[52]

Thomas Chalmers (1780–1847) pried apart the first two verses of Genesis to make room for the needed extra time. His approach is called the gap theory. Another approach understood each of the six days of creation as an age, thus vastly expanding the time frame of creation.[53] One negative reaction was published by Philip Gosse, a naturalist, but also a fundamentalist member of the Plymouth Brethren. In his *Omphalos: An Attempt to Untie the Geological Knot* (1857), he disagreed with the new geology, asserting rather that the semblance of change resulted from God's creating the world. He even suggested that God planted fossils to test faith.[54]

By the middle of the nineteenth century virtually everyone writing on the subject had accepted the earth's antiquity. Whether they subscribed to the gap theory or the day-age theory, or found loopholes in the genealogies preceding the flood story, they found a way to fit in the extra years. They also used the accommodation principle, suggesting that the Genesis stories had been accommodated to the viewpoint of the original audience.[55]

---

51. Ibid., 18–19.
52. Ronald L. Numbers, *The Creationists* (New York: Alfred A. Knopf, 1992), 4.
53. James R. Moore, "Geologists and Interpreters of Genesis in the Nineteenth Century," in *God and Nature,* ed. Lindberg and Numbers, 324–25.
54. Bratchell, *The Impact of Darwinism,* 105.
55. Moore, "Geologists and Interpreters of Genesis," 325.

Darwinism

Charles Darwin (1809–82) was born in England into a scientific family. His grandfather was a scientist, and his father was a physician. When young Darwin found medicine uncongenial, however, his father suggested that he prepare for the ministry.[56] Darwin began such a pursuit at Christ's College, where he met John Stevens Henslow (1796–1861), professor of botany at Cambridge and a fellow at Darwin's college. Henslow was also a clergyman, which was not an unusual combination at the time, and he fostered a love of science in Darwin.[57]

Darwin's views on evolution developed over a long period of time, culminating in his famous voyage on the *Beagle* (1831–36), which Henslow had arranged for him, and especially his visit to the Galapagos Islands, which gave him the material he needed to support his developing theory. Darwin's theory of evolution involved natural selection. Essentially he understood species to develop through changes occurring over time, the most useful of which increased survival and thus tended to be passed on to new generations while those changes that were not useful tended to die out. Although Darwin already had a draft of the plan of his first book, he did not publish *On the Origin of Species by Means of Natural Selection* until 1859, when it quickly sold out and created a storm of controversy. However, just as the story of Galileo is not the simple tale of ignorant religionists opposing enlightened scientists, so also the reaction to Darwin's seminal work was complex.

The response from the religious community was muted at first. More consternation arose about *Essays and Reviews* (1860), a book of nine essays that members of the clergy wrote approving of the new German higher biblical criticism. Only one essay dealt with Darwinism. In "On the Study of the Evidences of Christianity," Baden Powell (1796–1860) saw no conflict between science

---

56. A. Hunter Dupree, "Christianity and the Scientific Community in the Age of Darwin," in *God and Nature,* ed. Lindberg and Numbers, 351.

57. Owen Chadwick, *The Victorian Church: An Ecclesiastical History of England,* pt. 2 (London: Adam and Charles Black, 1970), 16.

and religion as long as they did not interfere with each other's spheres. He admired Darwin's work as laying down the principle of the self-evolving powers of nature through which God works.[58] English clerics had been dealing with the new geology since the turn of the century, and thus Darwin's *Origin* seemed like just another scientific work that needed to be considered.[59]

Nevertheless, the 1860s were generally quite a conservative period in England. Many religious people were opposed to Darwin's views and took positions that a few years later would be viewed as obscurantist. A famous story, almost as famous as Galileo's trial, occurred in 1860. At the annual meeting of the British Association for the Advancement of Science, at a meeting of the section on botany and zoology, J. W. Draper (who later wrote the famous *History of the Conflict between Religion and Science,* as mentioned earlier) was lecturing on the intellectual developments in Europe with special focus on Darwin's work. During the discussion, Samuel Wilberforce (1805–73), bishop of Oxford, was asked for his opinion. He argued that Darwin's theory was a hypothesis which, when tested, broke down. According to some accounts of the story, he asked Thomas Huxley about whether he believed that he was descended from apes. Huxley apparently replied,

If then, said I, the question is put to me "would I rather have a miserable ape for a grandfather or a man highly endowed by nature and possessed of great means and influence, and yet who employs those faculties and that influence for the mere purpose of introducing ridicule into a grave scientific discussion" — I unhesitatingly affirm my preference for the ape.

White, in his *History of the Warfare of Science with Theology In Christendom,* describes this exchange as a confrontation between

58. Bratchell, *The Impact of Darwinism,* 105.
59. Frederick Gregory, "The Impact of Darwinian Evolution on Protestant Theology," in *God and Nature,* ed. Lindberg and Numbers, 372–73.

science and theology.[60] However, Wilberforce's stated objection to Darwin's views was scientific rather than theological.

In 1867 Archbishop Denison denied that science was an equal partner with the Bible in the search for truth. He declared, "Those who accept the Bible do not investigate truth, they receive it." Some people responded with cries of "no, no," but others cheered.[61] In America the Episcopalian *American Quarterly Review* in 1865 suggested that "If Darwin's hypothesis is true, then the Bible is 'an unbearable fiction' and Christians have been duped by 'a monstrous lie' for nearly two thousand years."[62] Not all clergy were opposed, however. The views of Baden Powell, mentioned above, and John Henry Newman (1801–90) were typical of clergy who saw no problem with Darwin's views. John Henry (Cardinal) Newman, a member of the Oxford movement, was able in his *Apologia Pro Vita Sua* (1864) to reconcile the emerging scientific theories with his Christian belief.[63]

The majority of moderate-minded clergy reserved judgment. They would welcome scientific advances if they seemed sound but did not immediately accept every new idea. The moderates were concerned about a seeming disharmony between Darwinism and Genesis, but they were confident that if Darwin's views proved correct, then a way to reconcile them with biblical teaching would appear.[64] By 1871, when Darwin's *The Descent of Man* was published, the theory of evolution seemed probable or at least tolerable to most of the educated English population. The hypothesis that humans had developed from lower animals also seemed more probable than any other idea, not only to most scientists, but to educated members of the public. Even with its many problems and gaps, the idea was the best theory available.[65]

In America Darwin's views made little impact initially. In 1874, however, at an international meeting held in New York

60. Willem B. Drees, *Religion, Science, and Naturalism* (Cambridge and New York: Cambridge University Press, 1996), 65–66.
61. Chadwick, *The Victorian Church,* 25.
62. Gregory, "The Impact of Darwinian Evolution," 375–76.
63. Bratchell, *The Impact of Darwinism,* 127.
64. Chadwick, *The Victorian Church,* 27.
65. Ibid., 5.

of the Evangelical Alliance, an unscheduled floor debate occurred between the president of Princeton College, James McCosh (1811–94), and Charles Hodge (1797–1878), on the faculty at Princeton and the most influential Presbyterian theologian of the day. McCosh took the position that evolution could be reconciled with scripture. Hodge believed, to the contrary, that one had to make a choice between a world guided by God and one ruled by chance.[66]

The following year Hodge published his views in *What is Darwinism?* Hodge found it difficult to fathom the notion that something as intricate as the human eye, for example, could have been the result of natural laws operating without a guiding, intelligent, designing creator. A statement at the end of his book summed up his position: "The conclusion of the whole matter is that the denial of design in nature is virtually the denial of God." For Hodge, no middle ground existed.[67]

Other Protestants wanted to find the middle ground that Hodge denied. They wanted to find a way to reconcile Darwin's views with the Bible. The problem was not evolution, but natural selection, because it was based on chance variation. The liberals tended to agree with Hodge that natural selection was problematic, in spite of Darwin's own views on the matter, but they embraced evolution.[68] The most conservative of the reconcilers thought evolution would not drastically alter orthodox theology. Among these conservatives were James McCosh and A. H. Strong (1836–87). Other people were less concerned to preserve traditional formulations and more open to finding new ways of expressing theological truths. The Anglican clergyman Frederick Temple (1821–1902) was in this group. Still others made evolution the center of their theology. Most famous of these was Henry Ward Beecher (1818–87) and a group of Anglican clergy who published a sequel to *Essays and Reviews* called *Lux Mundi* (1889).[69]

Ironically, the attempt to reconcile evolution and Christian-

---

66. Gregory, "The Impact of Darwinian Evolution," 375–76.
67. Ibid., 376–77.
68. Ibid., 378–79.
69. Ibid.

ity depended on a rejection of natural selection, the very idea that distinguished Darwin's thought from others. A few writers, such as the American scientist Asa Gray (1810–88), believed that natural selection and a divinely ordered creation were not incompatible, but for the most part theologians did not try to reconcile natural selection and design.[70]

In Germany, thinkers such as Albrecht Ritschl (1822–89) and Rudolf Otto (1869–1937) offered a more radical solution to the problem. They thought that reconcilers such as McCosh were naive to believe in two realms, one natural and the other supernatural, that intersected each other. They saw Christianity as an ethical and social teaching derived from and related to human feeling, not as knowledge. They viewed its focus as human relationships with other humans rather than an understanding of the physical world. Nevertheless, they subordinated science to religion. People in the Ritschl-Otto nexus believed that learning about God and God's purposes through science was not possible, but that if coming from other sources, such knowledge was to be considered as taking precedence over scientific knowledge. Such thinking was not limited to Germany. Leslie Stephen (1832–1904) was willing to grant Darwin everything, because ultimately Darwin's theory was unimportant to him. He believed that religions thrive when they express our deepest feelings, not our abstract knowledge.[71]

By the end of World War I, most colleges in the American Midwest were teaching evolution. Even in the Southern Bible Belt, some church-affiliated schools taught evolution without a hint of trouble.[72] That situation changed rapidly, however, when after the war fundamentalists increasingly identified evolutionism as *the* culprit in the social ills that beset modern society.

A leading personality in this development was William Jennings Bryan (1860–1925), a Presbyterian layman and politician. For him the root of the problem was scripture. He declared that he would take one verse in Genesis over all that Darwin wrote. Bryan and other fundamentalists also objected to evolution on the

70. Ibid., 383.
71. Ibid., 383–87.
72. Numbers, *The Creationists,* 40.

grounds that it was only a theory, not a proven fact,[73] apparently not realizing that in science "theory" is the term used for the most strongly supported beliefs; nothing in science or any other human discipline is ever proven beyond a shadow of a doubt. They drew up lists of scientists who supposedly opposed evolution, but some of the scientists on their list were misrepresented, others were not biologists, and six were dead, two having died before Darwin's work was published. During the heyday of antievolutionary ferment, Albert Fleishmann (1862–1942), an obscure German zoologist who taught at the University of Erlangen in Bavaria, was one of very few reputable biologists who opposed evolution.[74]

Bryan objected for populist reasons to the teaching of evolution in schools. He did not like the idea of a minority of elitist scientists forcing their views on everybody else. In 1925 a high school teacher in Dayton, Tennessee, named John Thomas Scopes (1901–70) admitted that he had violated the recently passed ban in his state against teaching human evolution in order to test the constitutionality of the Tennessee antievolutionary law. His subsequent trial brought attention to the antievolution campaign and to William Jennings Bryan. Although Scopes lost the trial, the legal sparring did not end with the so-called monkey trial. In 1965 a young biology teacher in Little Rock, Arkansas, Susan Epperson (b. 1941) challenged the 1927 Arkansas law banning the teaching of evolution. The Supreme Court struck down the old statute in 1968.[75]

Next, creationists pushed for the inclusion of both creationism and evolution as alternate models. The state legislatures of Arkansas and Louisiana, as well as numerous local school boards, adopted the two-model approach. In 1982 the Supreme Court struck down the Arkansas law as unconstitutional. Three years later a Louisiana court reached a similar judgment, and in 1987 the Supreme Court upheld it. The Supreme Court acted as it did because in its view creationism was not science, but served only to advance religion.[76]

73. Ibid., 43–50.
74. Ibid., 51–52.
75. Ibid., 44, 243.
76. Ibid., 249–50.

The decision, however, left open the possibility of individual teachers voluntarily teaching creationism, and many teachers chose to do that. Polls revealed that anywhere from 30 percent (in Illinois) to 69 percent (in Kentucky) favored including creationism in the curriculum. How many actually did so (or do so) is not clear. Some parents who did not want their children to be taught evolution also turned to home schooling.[77] In addition, during the 1990s states have taken a number of steps to circumvent the Supreme Court rulings. Arizona, Alabama, Illinois, New Mexico, Texas, and Nebraska tried to remove evolution from state standards or to modify the teaching on this subject. Kansas, Illinois, Alabama, and Arizona removed the word "evolution" from their state science guidelines and substituted other terms such as "change over time," or added disclaimers to textbooks. Alabama's disclaimer was that "evolution is theory believed by some scientists, but not fact."[78]

At the time of this writing, as throughout the twentieth century, the majority of clergy in North American mainline denominations and many of their members have accepted Darwinism as the most likely theory of human origins. They interpret the story of Adam and Eve as symbolic rather than literally true. Nevertheless, a sizeable number of clergy and individuals in more conservative denominations continue to reject evolution, largely because it conflicts with a literal interpretation of scripture. Many of these people are not well educated, but some are highly educated. They are disturbed by questions that the present state of knowledge about human origins cannot answer.

Indeed, philosophers and theologians continue to debate many questions relating to the relationship between the physical and spiritual aspects of reality. Where these debates will lead is impossible to guess, but many thoughtful people will not likely return to the belief that a divine being created each species separately.

---

77. Ibid., 322.
78. People for the American Way Foundation, *Sabotaging Science: Creationist Strategy in the 90s* (*www.pfaw.org/issues/education/creationist-strategy.pdf*).

Christian Responses to Scientific Advances

Christians have reacted to scientific advances over the centuries, not simply as ignorant religionists resisting enlightened scientists. New scientific hypotheses have not emerged in completely developed form, acceptable to all scientists. Ridiculing people who did not have the foresight to understand that the new ideas would in time be accepted is easy in retrospect. Overly literal interpretations of scripture have, nevertheless, been a significant factor in resistance to scientific advances. This resistance has not hurt science so much as it has hurt religion. Churches often seem reactionary and unwilling to consider the possibility of new truth that might require a reexamination of old ways of thinking, including old ways of interpreting scripture. Protestants and Catholics both have been guilty of this refusal to rethink and reconsider.

Yet, how should Christians individually and corporately respond to scientific advances that seem to conflict with passages of scripture, especially when the scientific advances are in the realm of hypothesis rather than fully accepted theory? Must people of faith accept every new idea before it has become the consensus? Or should a period of waiting ensue until the evidence has mounted to the point of relative certainty? Or perhaps does a middle ground exist, where an idea is the most probable of all the models currently available, though not necessarily the clear consensus — a middle ground that should spur people concerned with Christian theology and ethics at least to begin exploring new interpretations and principles of interpretation?

Whichever course is followed, subjectivity is a problem. When does a hypothesis become the "best available" and by what criteria might a nonscientist make such a judgment? Individual Christians may come to their own conclusions based on their reading and perhaps personal acquaintance with scientists. But when denominations must make decisions — such as the ordination and blessing of sacred unions of homosexuals — that relate to scientific matters of this kind, the sensible course would seem to be to seek experts in the field for help.

Biblical scholars and theologians may help reinterpret passages that are or seem to be at odds with scientific advances, but scientists are the ones who can best articulate the scientific consensus. Rather than viewing scientists as antagonistic to the faith, people of faith should view scientists as seeking truth in the natural realm, just as Christians seek spiritual truth in the Bible. Of course, many scientists, such as coauthor Terry Hufford, are also Christian and thus are engaged in both searches.

If churches would approach the problems raised by scientific advances with the kind of middle course described above, the cause of truth would be advanced rather than hindered. In the process, Christians would make friends among people who are thoughtfully concerned about how to be spiritual in the contemporary world. Mistakes would still be made, but history demonstrates that in the past the mistakes of Christian biblical interpreters have more often been in the direction of being too slow to accept scientific advances rather than being too quick.

Without overreacting by going completely in the opposite direction, Christian interpreters can correct course and try to discern and embrace a fresh understanding of the truth. The basic principle is that the Bible teaches religion, not science. Although it touches on matters of a physical nature, the Bible does not do so in order to teach astronomy or biology or the like. The biblical authors and editors were primarily concerned with theological truth. Their view of the physical world sometimes is reflected but was not the point of their work.

The biblical authors were human; their scientific knowledge was limited to what was available in their time. Thoughtful Christians may affirm that God inspired them as to the spiritual content of their messages, but not the scientific. This affirmation is an updated version of the Augustinian principle of accommodation: God communicates with humans in language and concepts that they can understand.

Today, Christians do not tend to think of God as accommodating the divine message in the Bible to the modern hearers' cultural context. To the original hearers the ancient scientific worldview presupposed in the scriptures was familiar and therefore posed no problems. For contemporary readers, however, whom Christians believe the Spirit intends to address through the Bible as much as ancient readers, the biblical scientific worldview that conflicts with the modern one is a problem rather than a help. The old principle of accommodation, which worked well enough in the past, does not solve this difficulty. The difficulty is solved by the relatively recent realization that the human authors of the Bible had the usual limitations of finite mortals.

Thus, when generally accepted scientific advances seem to conflict with the words of scripture, Christians should take this state of affairs as a cue to reexamine the scriptural passages in question. What in one generation may seem like the crystal-clear, plain meaning of scripture may emerge in another generation as problematic. The more that is known about the physical world, the more difficult it is to relate ancient scripture with a prescientific perspective to contemporary life. Principles of interpretation make it easier to bridge the gap in a consistent fashion. One such principle is that spiritual truth and the reality of the physical world can never be in conflict. Thus, when reasonable certainty in a scientific matter has developed, the only responsible thing for Christians to do is to reexamine how the biblical passages that are or seem to be in conflict with the scientific advances are interpreted.

Following the central principle enunciated in this chapter, that the Bible is authoritative in matters of faith but not in matters of science, ironically upholds the authority of scripture. Failure to follow this principle undermines scripture's authority, for sooner or later people will accept the scientific truths. If the Bible seems to contradict science and this contradiction is not dealt with openly and honestly, the Bible's credibility will be diminished. The problem is not that the Bible is a lesser authority than science. In the realm of faith the Bible is, for Christians, the ultimate authority, but not in matters of science. Theology and science should complement each other. Science is not theology's enemy; they are friends because from time to time science forces Christians to reexamine their interpretive principles and in the process make important new discoveries about the Bible.

PRINCIPLES OF BIBLICAL INTERPRETATION

In chapter 1 we saw scientific evidence suggesting that homosexual orientation occurs naturally. In chapter 2 we learned that when science contradicts biblical interpretation, the time has come to reexamine interpretive principles and troublesome biblical passages. Before we turn our attention to the biblical passages themselves, in this chapter we examine traditional principles used to interpret the Bible in addition to those principles enunciated in chapter 2. We also look at ways in which the prophets, Jesus, and the apostles proclaimed new interpretations of scripture, which provide guidelines for offering fresh interpretations of scripture in our day.

"Hermeneutics" is a word that biblical scholars employ for the principles used to interpret texts. Among the most widely accepted traditional Christian hermeneutical precepts is that specific advice is read in light of general statements. Thus, Paul's advice to particular women in certain situations to keep silent in church (1 Cor. 14:34) is read in light of his more general statement that in Christ there is no male nor female (Gal. 3:28), which is part of the rationale for the ordination of women. Another principle is that texts in the Hebrew Scriptures are read in light of the New Testament. Thus the kosher laws prohibiting humans from eating pork and shellfish (Leviticus 11) are read by Christians in light of the New Testament rejection of these rules (Acts 11). Therefore, Christians do not feel constrained from eating ham, shrimp, and the like. Yet another principle is that the Epistles are interpreted in light of the Gospels. Some of the statements restricting women's roles in the Epistles are therefore considered in the light of Jesus' more affirming attitude toward women.

Hermeneutical Perspectives Related to Homosexuality

The Bible pays scant attention to homosexuality. Only two texts from the Hebrew Scriptures, Leviticus 18:22 and 20:13, speak directly, explicitly, generally, and unambiguously about male homosexual behavior. Genesis 19 and Judges 19 contain stories involving homosexual rape, but it is not obvious in these stories whether homosexuality in general, homosexual rape in particular, or a variety of evil behaviors is condemned. A number of texts in the Hebrew Scriptures also refer to religious functionaries whose role may have included homosexual intercourse, though this interpretation is far from certain. In addition, the story of Noah's son Ham uncovering him that leads to the curse of Ham's son Canaan (Gen. 9:22–25) may be a reference to homosexual incest. The stories of Jonathan and David and Ruth and Naomi are occasionally lifted up as positive homosexual relationships, though no explicit evidence is found in the narratives.

In the New Testament, words that may refer to male homosexuals are included in vice lists in 1 Corinthians 6:9 and 1 Timothy 1:10. Romans 1:26 probably refers to lesbianism, and Romans 1:27 includes a clear reference to male homosexuality. If Jesus ever said anything explicitly on the subject, no record remains. Nevertheless, hermeneutical principles may be drawn from what Jesus said on a variety of subjects.

When asked which commandment was the greatest, Jesus responded with an adaptation of the famous teaching from Deuteronomy 6:4–5 known in Judaism as the *Shema* (after the first Hebrew word in the passage), "Hear, O Israel: the Lord our God, the Lord is one; you shall love the Lord your God with all your heart, and with all your soul, and with all your mind, and with all your strength" (Mark 12:29–30; Matt. 22:37–38; Luke 10:27). The addition of the phrase "with all your mind" is a result of a difference in Hebrew and Hellenistic idiom. In traditional Hebrew anthropology, the term "heart" is not limited in meaning to emotions like love, but includes the will and intelligence as well. In order to convey the full meaning of the term in a context that was at least influenced by Hellenism, adding the word "mind" was necessary, making evident that love of God must be mindful as well as emotional.

The second commandment Jesus gives, "You shall love your neighbor as yourself" (Mark 12:31; Matt 22:39; Luke 10:25–28) comes from Leviticus 19:18. In Matthew's recounting of the story, Jesus goes on to say that "on these two commandments hang all the law and the prophets," suggesting that whatever cannot be derived from these two commandments is not essential. This statement does not, however, automatically annul provisions of the law that are repugnant to modern Western readers. Deriving the holiness rules in Leviticus — including prohibitions against wearing mixed fibers and the antihomosexuality rules as well as the kosher rules — from the first great commandment is possible on the assumption that loving God entails adherence to these rules. Surely the editors of Leviticus held this point of view,[1] and this perspective may have been Jesus' also.

Since Jesus affirmed that he came to fulfill the law rather than to abolish it (Matt. 5:17–20; Luke 16:17), his attitude toward the law was fundamentally positive, even if the Gospel writers interpreted Jesus' words in a more christological manner than he may have intended. In any case, Jesus' understanding of the law was not wooden or inflexible. He reinterpreted the written law[2] and the interpretive tradition surrounding it. Jesus said, "You have heard that it was said to those of ancient times.... But I say to you..." (Matt. 5:21–22). At times he even seemed to overturn the law, as when he rejected the eye-for-an-eye and tooth-for-a-tooth rule (Matt. 5:38–39; Luke 6:27–36; cf. Exod. 21:23–24; Lev. 24:19–20), though the intention of this rule was to limit retaliation. Since Jesus' alternative involves virtually limitless for-

---

1. Mary Douglas, *Leviticus as Literature* (Oxford: Oxford University Press, 1999).

2. Alan Watson, "Leviticus in Mark: Jesus' Attitude to the Law," in *Reading Leviticus: A Conversation with Mary Douglas,* ed. John F. A. Sawyer, Journal for the Study of the Old Testament Supplement Series 227 (Sheffield: Sheffield Academic Press, 1996), 269.

giveness, even here where Jesus seems to overthrow a law, Jesus' teaching is consistent with the spirit of the old written law. Jesus just took the ancient Hebrew concern to limit retaliation to even greater lengths.

In another incident Jesus reinterpreted the Sabbath law. When he and his disciples were passing through a field of grain on the Sabbath, they plucked some of the grain and ate it. The Pharisees chided them for disobeying the law (against working on the Sabbath). In response Jesus told the story about David and his companions who, when they were hungry, entered the Temple and ate the bread of the Presence, which only the priests were permitted to eat (1 Sam. 21:1–6). This citation was not a direct precedent, but an analogy. Then Jesus further justified his actions with the following principle, "The Sabbath was made for humankind, and not humankind for the Sabbath..." (Matt, 12:1–8; Mark 2:23–27; Luke 6:1–5). Similarly, when Jesus was confronted with the fact that he healed someone with a withered hand on the Sabbath, he asked a rhetorical question in response, "Is it lawful to do good or to do harm on the Sabbath, to save life or to kill" (Matt. 12:9–14; Mark 3:1–6; Luke 6:6–11; cf. John 5:1–18). In these cases, Jesus was not changing the written law which prescribes rest on the Sabbath. He was, however, challenging narrow interpretations of it.

On other occasions Jesus' reinterpretation of ancient laws is stricter rather than looser. For example, when asked about divorce, Jesus replies that Moses, understood as the human author of the law, had allowed a man to divorce his wife because of the hardness of human hearts (Deut. 24:1–4), but from the beginning such an action was not the intent of the law. He quotes Genesis 2:24, "For this reason a man shall leave his father and mother and be joined to his wife and the two shall become one flesh" (Mark 10:7–8; Matt. 19:5–6), and adds, "Therefore what God has joined together, let no one separate" (Mark 10:9; Matt. 19:6). Thus Jesus appeals to the story of creation as an even earlier and more sacred legal tradition than the Mosaic covenant. When asked about this teaching, he replies that anyone who divorces and remarries (another person) commits adultery (Mark 10:10–12; Luke 16:18; cf.

Matt. 5:31–32; Rom. 7:2–3; 1 Cor. 7:10–11). In the Matthean version of the story, an exception for adultery is allowed (the Greek term is *porneia*, meaning any kind of sexual immorality, though in the context adultery is implied — Matt. 5:31–32; 19:9). The point of this teaching is not to affirm heterosexuality as opposed to homosexuality. The point is to deny the validity of divorce except in certain extreme cases (and even the exception may be a later addition to Jesus' teaching, though Jesus may not have meant his response to be taken as a new law to be followed mindlessly).

In a case where Jesus is challenging the rabbinical exposition of a holiness (purity) law, the Gospel writers portray Jesus enunciating a more general principle. According to the story, Jesus is questioned about why his disciples do not wash their hands before eating, thus breaking the tradition of the elders (Matt. 15:2; Mark 7:2). Apparently the practice of hand washing before eating was an extension of the purity rules found in Leviticus. The concern was not primarily sanitation but ritual purity. After chastising the scribes and Pharisees for their hypocrisy, for Jesus apparently thought they were more concerned to uphold the human interpretive tradition than to obey the divine law, he responds to the specific concern by saying, "it is not what goes into the mouth that defiles a person, but it is what comes out of the mouth that defiles" (Matt. 15:11; Mark 7:15).

Expounding this principle, Jesus declares, "For out of the heart come evil intentions, murder, adultery, fornication, theft, false witness, slander. These are what defile a person, but to eat with unwashed hands does not defile" (Matt. 5:19–20; Mark 7:18–23). This principle suggests a different understanding of purity from the traditional Jewish one. Jesus may not have intended all the possible implications of this statement.[3] He was not a systematic theologian or ethicist. He was perhaps using the literary device known as hyperbole (exaggeration), just as Hosea did when, speaking for God, he said, "I desire mercy and not sacrifice" (Hos. 6:6). Hosea's point was probably that sacrifice was

3. Roger P. Booth, *Jesus and the Laws of Purity: Tradition History and Legal History in Mark 7,* Journal for the Study of the New Testament Supplement Series 13 (Sheffield: Sheffield Academic Press, 1986).

worthless if people did not live faithfully, rather than that sacrifice was utterly useless. Hosea's words perhaps made it easier for the exiled Jews of the sixth century B.C.E. to adjust to life in Babylon without a Temple and thus without sacrifices and also after the destruction of the Second Temple in 70 C.E., once again to a form of Judaism that did not include sacrifice.

Similarly, Jesus' meaning may have been that outward purity is worthless if inner purity is lacking. Nevertheless, Jesus' teaching in this and other similar incidents set the stage for the rejection of purity traditions by the early Christian community. Jesus was a Jew who affirmed the truth of divine law, but he understood both the written law and interpretations of that law in new ways. His understanding may not have made a radical break with the past but instead opened up that possibility for those who followed, just as Hosea's and other prophets' teachings did before him.

A Tradition of Reinterpretation

Many precedents for reinterpretation of tradition can be found in the Hebrew Scriptures. In the final chapters of the book of Isaiah are the words of a postexilic prophet known as Third Isaiah. He wrote:

> Do not let the foreigner joined to the LORD say,
>   "The LORD will surely separate me from his people";
> and do not let the eunuch say,
>   "I am just a dry tree."
> For thus says the LORD:
> To the eunuchs who keep my sabbaths,
>   who choose the things that please me
>   and hold fast my covenant,
> I will give, in my house and within my walls,
>   a monument and a name
>   better than sons and daughters;
> I will give them an everlasting name
>   that shall not be cut off.

> And the foreigners who join themselves to the LORD,
>   to minister to him, to love the name of the LORD,
>   and to be his servants,
> all who keep the sabbath, and do not profane it,
>   and hold fast my covenant —
> these I will bring to my holy mountain,
>   and make them joyful in my house of prayer;
> their burnt offerings and their sacrifices
>   will be accepted on my altar;
> for my house shall be called a house of prayer
>   for all peoples. (Isa. 56:3–8)

These words, written no earlier than the sixth century B.C.E., challenge the Deuteronomic laws that were codified much earlier, probably in the seventh century B.C.E.

> No one whose testicles are crushed or whose penis is cut off shall be admitted to the assembly of the LORD. (Deut. 23:1)

> No Ammonite or Moabite shall be admitted to the assembly of the LORD. Even to the tenth generation, none of their descendants shall be admitted to the assembly of the LORD, because they did not meet you with food and water on your journey out of Egypt, and because they hired against you Balaam son of Beor, from Pethor of Mesopotamia, to curse you. (Yet the LORD your God refused to heed Balaam; the LORD your God turned the curse into a blessing for you, because the LORD your God loved you.) You shall never promote their welfare or their prosperity as long as you live. (Deut. 23:3–6)

Deuteronomy 23:1 refers to the two operations that were used to produce the condition of a eunuch. The prohibition may have been related to the one in Deuteronomy 14:1 against disfiguring the body. The prohibition may also have been a reaction against religious practices involving sexual activity by eunuch-priests, although the evidence is scant.

In Isaiah 39:7, Isaiah of Jerusalem prophesies that some of Hezekiah's sons will become eunuchs in the palace of the king of

Babylon, thus destroying the royal line. In Isaiah 56:3–5 (quoted above) God abrogates a previous divine word regarding the unacceptability of eunuchs in order to thwart Babylon's purposes. Not only is the prohibition against eunuchs in the Israelite assembly overturned; the divine prophecy predicting Babylon's victory (Isa. 39:6) is undone. Babylon is victorious for a time, but that victory and Isaiah of Jerusalem's prophecy regarding it are not the final word. The divine word spoken by Third Isaiah is.[4]

The reasons Moabites and Ammonites were to be excluded is given in the text. They failed to provide sustenance when the Hebrews were passing through on their way out of Egypt, and they also hired Balaam to prophesy against them. Again, a new historical context may have prompted a new perspective. In any case approximately one hundred years after these two laws were originally codified, a postexilic prophet radically reinterpreted them, opening the doors for eunuchs and all foreigners to join the Jewish community so long as they observed the Sabbath, held fast to the covenant, and did the things that please God.[5]

Not only did a postexilic prophet reinterpret the Deuteronomic law; the author of the book of Ruth may have done the same thing in a more subtle fashion. Although scholars are divided as to whether Ruth is a historical story told sometime after David's reign or a short story written in the postexilic period, the fact remains that in this story David is presented as the fourth-generation descendant of Ruth, a Moabite woman. For the editors of Deuteronomy to include a law that excluded King David himself from membership in the group over which he ruled as king would seem odd. If the book of Ruth was written before David's birth and the genealogy added later, or if the whole book was written within a reasonable period after David's reign, then this story would have been known when the Deuteronomic laws were codified in the seventh century B.C.E.

---

4. Frederick J. Gaiser, "A New Word on Homosexuality? Isa 56:1–8 as Case Study," *Word and World* 14 (Summer 1994): 282–88.

5. See Odil Hannes Steck, *The Prophetic Books and Their Theological Witness,* trans. James D. Nogalski (St. Louis: Chalice Press, 1996).

More likely the story was written as protest literature during the postexilic period when Ezra and Nehemiah were enforcing the Deuteronomic laws excluding foreigners by requiring Jewish men married to foreign women to send their foreign wives and "half-breed" children away (Ezra 9:1–10:44; Neh. 13:3; cf. Neh. 10:30; Deut. 7:1–6).[6] Jonah is another biblical book that may have been written in protest of narrowly exclusive laws. Esther with its ridicule of the laws of the Persians — which could not be changed, even by the king — may also be read in part as a protest against an overly rigid Jewish understanding of law. Although doubt exists about the motivations, literary genre, and dating of Ruth, Jonah, and Esther, general agreement exists about the text from Isaiah 56. Its vision of the Jewish community is more inclusive than the one presented in Deuteronomy.

Thus, Jesus' reinterpretation of laws and interpretations of laws continues a tradition already well established in the Hebrew Bible. Both the principle he enunciated — that what comes out of the mouth is defiling rather than what enters it — and the interpretation of it he gave (although focused on the specific issue of hand washing before eating) form the basis for the Christian replacement of the Levitical ritual purity system, which is externally focused, with an understanding of purity that is much more internally based. Whether Jesus would have followed this principle to all of its logical conclusions is doubtful. However, that question does not invalidate the application of his principle in new contexts. What is a matter mostly of logical inference in Jesus' teaching becomes explicit in the teaching of Jesus' apostles.

The Teaching of the Apostles

In Acts 11 Peter is criticized by the Jewish Christians in Jerusalem for visiting and eating with uncircumcised men. He then recounts a vision in which he sees a variety of unclean animals. In the vision a voice tells him to get up, kill, and eat. Peter, understanding

---

6. André LaCocque, *The Feminine Unconventional: Four Subversive Figures in Israel's Tradition* (Minneapolis: Fortress, 1990), 84–116.

the voice to be God's, responds that he cannot because nothing unclean or profane has ever entered his mouth. Then Peter is told that what God has made clean Peter must not call profane. This dialogue is repeated twice more. Peter continues by explaining that after the visionary experience three men came to him and the Spirit told him to go with them and not to make any distinction between the uncircumcised men and those who had been circumcised.

In the context in which it is reported, the vision is intended as divine justification for acceptance of noncircumcised Gentiles into the Christian community. The Gentiles were considered unclean, just like the animals in the vision. Just as Jesus' teaching on hand washing provides a more generally applicable principle, this vision also suggests a broader principle, certainly indicating that the kosher laws were to be left behind. Probably also in general, the Jewish purity laws that separated Jews from Gentiles were implicitly not binding on Christians.

Paul is in agreement with Peter that circumcision is not required for Gentile Christians. He writes in Romans 2:25–29,

> Circumcision indeed is of value if you obey the law; but if you break the law, your circumcision has become uncircumcision. So, if those who are uncircumcised keep the requirements of the law, will not their uncircumcision be regarded as circumcision? Then those who are physically uncircumcised but keep the law will condemn you that have the written code and circumcision but break the law. For a person is not a Jew who is one outwardly, nor is true circumcision something external and physical. Rather, a person is a Jew who is one inwardly, and real circumcision is a matter of the heart — it is spiritual and not literal. Such a person receives praise not from others but from God.

Much of Paul's writing sounds very negative about the law. For example, in Romans 6:14, he writes, "For sin will have no dominion over you, since you are not under law but under grace." However, in Romans 7:6, he appears to reject the old written code of law rather than divine law: "But now we are discharged from the law, dead to that which held us captive, so that we are slaves not under the old written code but in the new life of the Spirit."

In a similar vein, the author of Hebrews recalls Jeremiah's prophecy of the new covenant (Jer. 31:31–34):

> Jesus has now obtained a more excellent ministry, and to that degree he is the mediator of a better covenant, which has been enacted through better promises. For if that first covenant had been faultless, there would have been no need to look for a second one. (Heb. 8:6–7)

He then cites Jeremiah's famous words (slightly adapted):

> The days are surely coming, says the Lord,
>> when I will establish a new covenant with the house of Israel
>> and with the house of Judah;
> not like the covenant that I made with their ancestors,
>> on the day when I took them by the hand to lead them out of the land of Egypt;
> for they did not continue in my covenant,
>> and so I had no concern for them, says the Lord.
> This is the covenant that I will make with the house of Israel
>> after those days, says the Lord:
> I will put my laws in their minds,
>> and write them on their hearts,
> and I will be their God,
>> and they shall be my people,
> And they shall not teach one another
>> or say to each other, "Know the Lord,"
> for they shall all know me,
>> from the least of them to the greatest.
> For I will be merciful toward their iniquities,
>> and I will remember their sins no more." (Heb. 8:8–12)

The author of Hebrews then interprets these words: "In speaking of a 'new covenant,' he has made the first one obsolete. And what is obsolete and growing old will soon disappear" (Heb. 8:13).

In quoting Jeremiah, the author of Hebrews uses the Greek translation with slight adaptations. This translation brings out a nuance that is implicit in the Hebrew, but which would not show up in the Greek without making it explicit. Whereas Jeremiah says, "I will put my law within them and I will write it on their hearts," the text in Hebrews reads, "I will put my laws in their *minds,* and write them on their hearts" (Heb. 8:10, emphasis added). A similar adaptation in Jesus' quotation of Deuteronomy 4:5–6, the *Shema,* has already been noted. In Hebrew the term "heart" is used in much the same way the Greeks and we today use the term "mind." The heart was considered the seat of intelligence and the will, not simply emotions such as love. The implication is that the new covenant that the author of Hebrews understands Jesus to have inaugurated will no longer require rote obedience to external laws; rather, thoughtful understanding of what God desires of humans is required. Admittedly, the focus of the author of Hebrews is elsewhere. Nevertheless, his use of words suggests this interpretation.

Jeremiah was not rejecting the Jewish law; he was, however, reemphasizing what was perhaps always a part of the Hebrew tradition: the law must be internalized, not simply followed in a wooden fashion. The author of Hebrews may have understood this prophecy in the light of Jesus' practice of thinking through the rationales for legal requirements rather than simply following the externally codified law, and even if he was not consciously thinking in these terms, this way of relating the new covenant to Jesus' life and teaching is natural.

When the reference to the new covenant in Hebrews is combined with Paul's contrast between the written law code and the spirit, the implication is that human words can never completely capture eternal sacred law. At best, law codes present a temporary, culturally bound expression of the divine law. One thing is evident: the Christian concept of the new covenant is not a new set of laws but rather is a fundamentally different way of conceptualizing divine law. The implication is that any ethical rules in the Bible, whether in the Hebrew Scriptures or New Testament, are provisional guidelines that may or may not be valid for all times in all places. Principles such as reverence for life are eternally valid. Particular manifestations of such principles — as, for example, the ancient Hebrew blood taboos — may not be.

Model Interpreters

Biblical authors in both testaments, but especially Jesus, Peter, Paul, and the author of Hebrews, should be lifted up as model interpreters. They revered the religious law, but they also reinterpreted it — at times rather radically. If people of faith cannot use the Bible to find role models for interpretation of the Bible, where else should role models be sought?[7] The suggestion that Christians should emulate Jesus may seem to some the epitome of arrogance. Jesus, after all, was the Christ, they contend. How dare anyone presume to fill his shoes? This objection is serious. However, Jesus was not the only biblical figure who reinterpreted laws. The postexilic poet who wrote Isaiah 56 stood before him, and Peter, Paul, and the author of Hebrews stood after him, all doing the same thing. The objection may still be raised that all of these biblical authors were operating on a totally different plane than people of faith do today. Do contemporary Christians have the right to follow their lead?

No simple answer to this question is available. However, when Jesus' disciples asked him to teach them to pray, he did not give them a prayer to memorize and repeat, in spite of the fact that Christians have done exactly this with the Lord's Prayer. Quite the contrary, he gave them a model of prayer. In the Matthean version, which probably preserves the more authentic introduction, he said, "Pray then *in this way...*" (Matt. 6:9; Luke 11:2; emphasis added). He trusted his disciples to construct their own prayers. He rarely gave specific ethical rules; usually his advice was both more demanding and more general than simple do's and don'ts. Thus, the understanding of the new covenant found

---

7. For similar views, see Brian K. Blount, "Reading and Understanding the New Testament on Homosexuality," in *Homosexuality and Christian Community,* ed. C. L. Seow (Louisville, Ky.: Westminster/John Knox Press, 1996), 30–31; Gaiser, "A New Word on Homosexuality," 280–93.

in the book of Hebrews in concert with the interpretive practices of the biblical authors leads to following Jesus' mindful example rather than mindlessly following even his specific advice or that of other biblical authors.

Finally, if Christians do not adopt such an approach, on what grounds can Jesus' very specific instructions on divorce be reinterpreted as most churches have done? Jesus said that anyone who divorces and marries a new spouse, except perhaps when some sort of sexual immorality has occurred, is committing adultery. These words are strong. Rotely following what Jesus said would make divorce impossible in many cases where it seems necessary today for the health of one or both parties, as when a pattern of abuse exists.

Looking at Jesus' words in their historical context, sensitive readers see that the Jewish law allowed men to divorce their wives for very minor causes. In that society a divorced woman who could not return to her father's house was in a terrible economic bind. On one level Jesus was probably responding to husbands' callous disregard for their wives' well-being. On a deeper level he was understanding the purpose of marriage, which he believed to be a lifelong partnership in which two people bond with one another. In Jesus' day, easy divorces left women vulnerable. Today the inability to divorce would subject some women (and men) to terrible abuse, both physical and mental. Thus, although most Christians affirm Jesus' understanding of marriage, out of compassion for individuals most Christian denominations allow divorce. In so doing they are following the spirit of Jesus' message rather than the letter of his teaching.

Finally, although the Bible's own implicit teaching on how the Bible should be used is to be given greater weight than subsequent interpretations, Protestant Christians should note the attitude of the Protestant reformers. Luther understood how the letter kills, but the Spirit gives life (2 Cor. 3:6), so he believed that the gospel is not finally a written word, but an oral one. In his *Theses Concerning Faith and Law* (1535), he argues that if Christians have Christ, they can establish new laws as Paul, Peter, and most importantly Jesus did. Aware of the dangers of such a statement, Luther adds that individuals do not have the authority to establish new laws, but the universal church does.[8]

Luther was no more able to receive a hearing before the universal church (a Church Council in his day) than we are today. Yet his concern that the freedom to establish new laws be understood as a corporate rather than an individual one is important. Individuals may allow self-interest to color their understanding. Congregations, consisting of many individuals, and denominations, consisting of many congregations, are less prone to this problem. As churches struggle to respond faithfully to God's will, individuals contribute to the discussion, but ultimately church bodies must make the decisions that will govern those bodies on matters of church membership, ordination, and the like.

For John Calvin the believer's duty is to follow God's will, not simply the commandments in the Bible, though for Calvin the written word and the divine will are unified. Nevertheless, Calvin was not a literalist. The first chapter of this book discusses his approach to dealing with biblical passages in which the scientific viewpoints of the biblical authors were out of date. He used the principle of accommodation[9] (discussed in our chapter 2). Of course the issues were cosmological and therefore did not involve matters of morality. The manner in which Calvin would interpret a passage that touches on an ethical issue, yet may be based on an outmoded scientific concept, is not certain. He would surely find the matter troubling. We do not know how he would react, but we can respond according to his model and treat it as the rare case of the biblical author's understanding of the divine will on a matter involving morality being limited by his own human ignorance. This approach would be consistent with Calvin's way of dealing with questions that confronted him. As we turn our attention to texts that have been studied in relation to homosexuality, we keep in mind the principles of biblical interpretation that have across the centuries developed for dealing with troubling texts.

---

8. Gaiser, "A New Word on Homosexuality," 288–90.
9. See I. John Hesselink, *Calvin's Concept of the Law,* Princeton Theological Monograph Series 30 (Allison Park, Pa.: Pickwick Publications, 1992), esp. his "Conclusion: Calvin's Dynamic Understanding of the Law," 277–86.

chapter four _____

NEW APPROACHES
TO ANCIENT TEXTS

In our final chapter, we take an in-depth look at the biblical
texts that are relevant to a discussion of homosexuality, using
the principles of interpretation discussed in the previous two
chapters. In doing so, we carefully consider the historical and
cultural influences that may have shaped biblical understandings
of homosexuality as well as the broader context of biblical teachings. Finally, we propose an interpretive approach for dealing with
the biblical material related to homosexuality.

Before considering the biblical texts related to what we today call homosexuality, we remind ourselves of the history of the
word, which was discussed in chapter 1. "Homosexual" is of relatively recent origin; the term was coined in the nineteenth century
by a Hungarian physician and used in English for the first time
in 1912.[1] The phenomena to which the term refers, however, are
ancient, although the ancients did not necessarily conceptualize
sexuality in the same way that moderns do. The contemporary
view that separates orientation from behavior was apparently unknown in biblical times. Although biblical authors did not think
about same-gender sexual behavior as moderns do (which af-
fects interpretation of ancient texts), the fundamental reality of
sexual behavior between persons of the same gender was part of
their world.

---

1. R. W. Burchfield, ed. *A Supplement to the Oxford English Dictionary,* vol. 2 (Oxford:
Clarendon, 1976), 136.

Creation and (Homo)Sexuality

The creation stories in Genesis 1 and 2 are often thought to have relevance for the question of the Bible's teaching on homosexuality. These stories do not speak directly about homosexuality, but they are concerned with sexual relations between men and women. The implications that may be drawn from these passages for same-sex relationships are the issue here.

Genesis 1 tells the familiar story of the six days of creation followed by the seventh day of rest. The Deity's final creative act in this story is the creation of humanity in God's own image, male and female (Gen. 1:27). God goes on to instruct the humans to "be fruitful and multiply . . . " (Gen. 1:28). Heterosexual intercourse is the means through which this injunction will be fulfilled.

Some interpreters see this story as providing the only acceptable model for humans. The statement of James R. Edwards is a typical example:

> The argument that homosexuality is a God-given orientation or lifestyle, as is commonly asserted today, cannot be considered apart from reference to the order of creation in Genesis 1–2. Genesis 1:26 states that humanity is created in the image of God, and that being male and female reflect that image. . . . God created the human race not in uniformity, but of complementary sexes, male and female, whose union is described as "one flesh." Heterosexual union, as guarded and preserved in the covenant of marriage, is not simply a human choice or one variety of sexual union among many, but an order of creation. It is a holy vocation in the sense that only this form of union allows humanity to fulfill God's command to "be fruitful and multiply" (Gen. 1:28). Male and female thus find their mutual fulfillment, as well as their procreative function, in that complementary opposite, a teaching that is reaffirmed in the New Testament in Matthew 19:5; Mark 10:6–8; and 1 Corinthians 11:7–9.[2]

---

2. James R. Edwards, "The Bible and the Practice of Homosexuality," *Theology Matters* (May/June 1995): 12.

However, if heterosexual union is the only "holy vocation," how would Jeremiah, Jesus, and Paul, none of whom married, be accommodated to the model? Logically, the model is the typical pattern for humans, not the only acceptable one, though a safe assumption is that the ancient Hebrews preferred this pattern. In the ancient biblical world, where farming was the main economic activity and many children were required in order to provide enough labor, the command to be fruitful and multiply (Gen. 1:28) certainly made a great deal of sense. In an overcrowded contemporary world, following this rule literally would lead to serious problems.

Similarly, Genesis 2:24, "a man leaves his father and his mother and clings to his wife, and they become one flesh," is a poetic description of an intimate relationship between two adults who bond with each other physically and presumably emotionally as well. Usually, the two adults are a man and a woman. If they happen to be two men or two women, is that logically any more of a problem than if a man remains single? Richard Whitaker suggests that the biblical author presumed that procreation was the primary purpose of sexual relationships, but believes that this assumption needs to be reexamined in light of contemporary concerns.[3] Victor Furnish points out that the text does not explicitly require monogamy, nor even directly mention marriage! Perhaps in the context of the Hebrew Scriptures, reading in these meanings is fair; however, the patriarchs were polygamous and not condemned for their sexual pattern.[4]

Jesus refers to Genesis 2:24 when he comments on divorce, thus signaling his approval of the verse (Mark 10:7–9; Matt. 19:5–6). However, his use of it as a justification for his own teaching against divorce no more suggests that heterosexual marriage is the only acceptable model of human intimate relationships than

---

3. Richard E. Whitaker, "Creation and Human Sexuality" in *Homosexuality and Christian Community,* ed. C. L. Seow (Louisville, Ky.: Westminster/John Knox Press, 1996), 3–13.

4. Victor Paul Furnish, "The Bible and Homosexuality: Reading the Texts in Context," in *Homosexuality in the Church,* ed. Jeffrey S. Siker (Louisville, Ky.: Westminster/John Knox Press, 1994), 21–22.

the original teaching itself does. Since Jesus was single, he himself did not fit the pattern. His point was that marriage is intended as a lifetime partnership, not that everyone must be married (cf. Matt. 19:10–11). He was perhaps concerned with the welfare of women who were casually tossed aside by husbands who no longer found them useful. We have no way of knowing whether the question of same-sex marriage ever confronted Jesus. His words on marriage, however, do not logically exclude the possibility of lifetime homosexual partnerships any more than they exclude the acceptability of single adults. This interpretation is not to say that Jesus was in favor of homosexuality, only that his words cannot be construed as a condemnation of it.

Genesis 19 (and Judges 19)

Of all the passages that contain (or are thought to contain) references to homosexuality, the story of Sodom and Gomorrah is perhaps the most famous. Nevertheless, a careful reading shows that the story is the least useful for discussions of what kinds of sexual behavior are appropriate between consenting males. Genesis 19, and the related Judges 19, both deal with attempted homosexual *rape.* Yd', the Hebrew verb used of the intentions of the men of Sodom (Genesis 19) and Gibeah (Judges 19) regarding the strangers, has the root meaning of "to know," but this word is sometimes used of sexual intercourse. In light of Lot's horrified reaction to the request and his offer of his virgin daughters as a substitute and the similar substitution of the Levite's concubine in Judges 19 that results in her rape and murder, understanding the verb in its sexual meaning probably makes sense. The arguments of Derrick Sherwin Bailey[5] and John Boswell,[6] who relies on Bailey — that the Sodomites simply want to get acquainted — are not convincing. The context of both this story

5. Derrick Sherwin Bailey, *Homosexuality and the Western Christian Tradition* (London: Longmans, Green and Co., 1955), 1–28.

6. John Boswell, *Christianity, Social Tolerance, and Homosexuality: Gay People in Western Europe from the Beginning of the Christian Era to the Fourteenth Century* (Chicago: University of Chicago Press, 1980), 93–94.

and the parallel one in Judges 19 is too suggestive of a sexual meaning to read the verb in its nonsexual denotation. The residents do not simply want to get to know the strangers; they want to rape them. Whether the intended rape in Genesis 19 was the sole or primary factor that caused God to annihilate the cities, as is discussed below, does not matter much. Similarly, whether the motivations of the men of Sodom were inhospitality,[7] humiliation of suspicious strangers,[8] or satisfaction of lust (homosexual or heterosexual),[9] or even some combination of these[10] does not alter the reality that the intended sexual behavior was coercive. Since sex and violence are inextricably tied together in this story, even if the punishment came in part as a result of the residents' attempt to rape the strangers, which seems likely, we cannot be sure whether the divine wrath was a result of the homosexual nature of the rape or simply the brutal personal violence directed at innocent strangers. For this reason, the story cannot easily be used in contemporary discussions of the propriety of sexual intercourse between consenting persons of the same gender.[11]

Given the context of the Genesis story in which angels have been dispatched to Sodom to discover whether enough good men live there to dissuade God from destroying the place, the intended actions of the residents against the angels (whom they think are ordinary men, not angels) are presumably not the only reason

---

7. See Bailey, *Homosexuality and the Western Christian Tradition*, 1–8; Boswell, *Christianity, Social Tolerance, and Homosexuality*, 91–98; D. A. Helminiak, *What the Bible Really Says about Homosexuality* (San Francisco: Alamo Square Press, 1994), 35–41; Weston W. Fields, *Sodom and Gomorrah: History and Motif in Biblical Narrative* (Sheffield: Sheffield Academic Press, 1997), 231.

8. See Helminiak, *What the Bible Really Says*, 38–39; Ken Stone, "Gender and Homosexuality in Judges 19: Subject-Honor, Object Shame?" *Journal for the Study of the Old Testament* 67 (1995): 87–107; Fields, *Sodom and Gomorrah*.

9. Claus Westermann, John J. Scullion, S.J., trans., *Genesis 12–16, A Commentary* (Minneapolis: Augsburg Press, 1985), 301.

10. See especially J. A. Loader, *A Tale of Two Cities: Sodom and Gomorrah in the Old Testament, Early Jewish and Early Christian Traditions*, Contributions to Biblical Exegesis and Theology 1 (Kampen: J. H. Kok, 1990), 37.

11. Richard B. Hays, "Awaiting the Redemption of Our Bodies," in *Homosexuality in the Church*, ed. Siker, 5–6; Choon-Leong Seow, "A Heterotextual Perspective," 15–16, and "Textual Orientation," in *Biblical Ethics and Homosexuality: Listening to Scripture*, ed. Robert L. Brawley (Louisville, Ky.: Westminster/John Knox Press, 1996), 21–24.

that God decides to destroy the place, though their behavior could easily have confirmed the divine suspicions about the city of ill repute.

Fortunately, we have the witness of many ancient biblical authors to help interpret this story, especially in regard to the nature of the sins that elicited God's displeasure. Of all the later biblical references to this story, none refers explicitly to what moderns call homosexuality as the sin. In Isaiah 1:1-11, vain sacrifices and general iniquity are cited; in Jeremiah 23:14, adultery and lies; in Ezekiel 16:44, 49–50, haughtiness and abomination. In the apocryphal book Sirach, the reason given is arrogance (16:8) and in another apocryphal book, Wisdom of Solomon, it is wickedness and inhospitality (10:6–8; 19:13–14). In the New Testament, Sodom and Gomorrah are symbols of divine judgment (Matt. 10:15; 11:23–24; Luke 10:12; 17:29; Rom. 9:29).[12]

The meaning of two additional references is not immediately obvious. Jude 6–7 reads:

> And the angels who did not keep their own position, but left their proper dwelling, he has kept in eternal chains in deepest darkness for the judgment of the great Day. Likewise, Sodom and Gomorrah and the surrounding cities, which, in the same manner as they, indulged in sexual immorality and pursued unnatural lust, serve as an example by undergoing a punishment of eternal fire.

The reference in Jude 6 to the angels not keeping their own position is an allusion to the story in Genesis 6:4 of the sons of God, i.e. angels or the like, cohabiting with human women. In a Pseudepigraphal work, the Testament of Naphtali, this same connection is made between Sodom and the story in Genesis 6, but more explicitly.

> The Gentiles went astray, and forsook the Lord, and changed their order and obeyed sticks and stones, spirits of deceit.

---

12. Marion L. Soards, *Scripture and Homosexuality: Biblical Authority and the Church Today* (Louisville, Ky.: Westminster/John Knox Press, 1995), 16.

But ye shall not be so, my children, recognizing in the fir-
mament, in the earth, and in the sea, and in all created
things, the Lord who made all things, that ye become not as
Sodom, which changed the order of nature. In like manner
the watchers also changed the order of their nature, whom
the Lord cursed at the flood. . . .

Thus, the phrase in Jude 7, "sexual immorality and unnatural
lust," was probably intended to refer to men's lust for angels
rather than for mortals of the same gender, though the latter
possibility cannot be excluded, nor can a combination of both
concerns.

The same strange story in Genesis 6:4 is also perhaps con-
nected obliquely with the reference to Sodom and Gomorrah in
2 Peter 2:4–10. Not until the postbiblical period were the first
unambiguous condemnations of the residents of Sodom for their
homosexual behavior written by the Jews Philo and Josephus.[13]
Their views are considered below.

Today, the commonly accepted view is that rape is a crime involving primarily hunger for power, and only secondarily lust.
Reading between the lines, the reason the men of Sodom all
wanted to "know" the strangers that were staying with Lot
was likely that the Sodomites were fearful that the strangers
might be spies or otherwise planning to do them harm. The
best defense is often a good offense and so the citizens probably
intended to humiliate the men by homosexually raping them,
thus symbolically turning them into women. (The negative view
of women underlying this form of humiliation should not be
missed.) Such behavior would obviously have been an extreme
form of inhospitality.

The same concern seems to have been the motivation in the
similar story in Judges 19 where a Levite from Ephraim is travel-
ing with his concubine and finds lodging with a fellow Ephraimite

13. Victor Paul Furnish, "The Bible and Homosexuality: Reading the Texts in
Context," 19–20; Seow, "A Heterotextual Perspective," 15–16, and "Textual Orien-
tation," 22; cf. Calum Carmichael, *Law, Legend, and Incest in the Bible: Leviticus 18–20*
(Ithaca, N.Y.: Cornell University Press, 1997), 53–55.

who resides in Gibeah. Again the men of the town come pounding on the door, wanting to "know" the stranger. Just as in the Sodom and Gomorrah story where Lot offered his two virgin daughters instead of the angels (in his mind, raping them would have apparently been a lesser evil), so in this story the householder's daughter and the Levite's concubine are offered. The concubine is accepted, gang-raped, and murdered. Apparently, she was considered to be the Levite's property. Thus, raping her would have sent the same message to the Levite as raping him — that he was not welcome — though the stronger warning would have been delivered to the Levite in person. However, the fact that the men accepted a female substitute is an indication that homosexual sex was not their object; violence was. The fact that the Sodomites rejected the women whom Lot offered as substitutes does not contradict this conclusion. Lot's daughters did not belong to the stranger; to rape them would thus not harm him. The Levite's concubine did belong to the Levite, and thus her rape and murder directly affected him.

Even if this analysis is viewed as wrong and all the men of Sodom and Gibeah were presumably lusting homosexually after the strangers, which seems unlikely especially since the men of Gibeah accept the concubine, the intended behavior is still rape. Rape of any sort is evil. In addition, according to the biblical interpretations of this story, the primary reasons that Sodom and Gomorrah were punished were more general than this one incident. Thus, Genesis 19 and Judges 19 do not contribute to an understanding of what the Bible says about sexual intercourse between consenting adults of the same gender, because too many variables reside in these accounts.

Leviticus 18:22 and 20:13

Leviticus 18:22 reads, "You shall not lie with a male as with a woman; it is an abomination." The verse is implicitly addressed to male readers, emphatically prohibiting males from having anal intercourse with other males; such activity is an abomination. The penalty, given in Leviticus 20:13, is death.

The Hebrew term translated as "abomination," *to'ebah,* found in Leviticus 18:22, is used of anything considered unacceptable behavior, including both what today are considered cultic, ritual "sins" and what are viewed as moral wrongs. For example, in Deuteronomy 7:26 the term is used of gold and silver idols; however, in Deuteronomy 25:16 it is used of dishonest weights.[14] Thus, in and of itself the term "abomination" does not tell us whether the ancient Hebrew author of this text thought male homosexual intercourse was morally wrong or a ritual violation, or whether he would have even understood the distinction, which was not made by the ancient Hebrews, at least not originally.[15]

The Reformed Christian tradition makes a distinction between moral and cultic sins because of the New Testament's rejection of circumcision and dietary laws, both of which have been considered cultic rather than moral. The New Testament authors may not have thought of this distinction in this fashion. What the New Testament authors explicitly rejected were those provisions of the Mosaic law that were specifically Jewish and that separated Jews and Gentiles. That distinction is not the same as one between moral and cultic laws.

The Holiness Code (Leviticus 17–26), in which Leviticus 18:22 and 20:13 appear, contains a variety of prohibitions, some evidently ritual in nature, such as various provisions relating to sacrificial rites (Leviticus 17), and some clearly ethical, such as reiterations and elaborations of some of the ten commandments (Lev. 19:11–16). And there are some that even we moderns might have difficulty determining whether they are of a moral or cultic nature, such as prohibitions against eating the fruit of a tree until its fifth year (Lev. 19:23–25).

Included in the Holiness Code are prohibitions against wearing fabric of mixed fibers and sowing two different kinds of seed in the same field (Lev. 19:19) and having sex with a menstruating

---

14. Seow, "A Heterotextual Perspective," 14.

15. Jacob Neusner, *The Idea of Purity in Ancient Judaism,* Studies in Judaism in Late Antiquity, vol. 1 (Leiden: E. J. Brill, 1973), 1–2; cf. Hyam Maccoby, *Ritual and Morality: The Ritual Purity System and Its Place in Judaism* (Cambridge: Cambridge University Press, 1999).

woman (Lev. 18:19). Are these cultic or are they moral violations? The answer is not obvious, because the question is misguided, superimposing modern categories on an ancient text. To understand the ancient perspective on the material in the Holiness Code in particular and Leviticus in general, interpreters should look first to the text itself.[16]

The biblical authors of the Holiness Code indicate that the reason the Hebrews were to avoid the behaviors outlined in the code was because they were to distinguish themselves from their Egyptian and Canaanite neighbors (Lev. 18:2–3, 24–29). This reason might suggest that the antihomosexuality law was focused on the worship practices of their neighbors, rather than homosexuality in general; this suggestion is possible, though not certain. The term *to'ebah*, "abomination," is frequently used in cultic contexts, especially of strange customs associated with worship of pagan gods. In the context of Leviticus 18 in which child sacrifice is included, perhaps the focus was on some sort of homosexual behavior that was part of a worship service, though this possibility is uncertain.[17]

The Holiness Code outlined a way of life that was understood to be pleasing to God. In Leviticus 19:1–2, the Lord spoke to Moses telling him to declare to the people that because God is holy, the people also should be holy. The words "holy" and "holiness" from the Hebrew root *qdsh* did not mean precisely the same thing to the ancient Hebrews that they mean to us today. Holiness was understood to be a positive condition consistent with God that various kinds of impurity could threaten. To be holy was to be pure, and to be pure was to be ritually clean as well as morally clean, though again the distinction is a modern one. The origins of the classifications are obscure. Anthropologist Mary Douglas suggests that all of these terms may ultimately emerge from an ancient sense of order and classification quite foreign to modern

16. Sarah J. Melcher, "The Holiness Code and Human Sexuality," in Brawley, ed., *Biblical Ethics and Homosexuality,* 87–102.

17. Martti Nissinen, *Homoeroticism in the Biblical World,* trans. Kirsi Stjerna (Minneapolis: Fortress Press, 2000), 39.

sensibilities. Something was clean or pure if it conformed to the accepted ideas about how the world was structured.[18]

A well-known example of the division into clean and unclean is found in the Leviticus 11. These kosher laws indicate which animals were considered clean or unclean. They are not part of the Holiness Code but are cut out of much the same cloth; indeed the same people who were responsible for the Holiness Code may have edited these passages.[19] The basis for the animal divisions was not primarily hygienic. Cleanliness was not about sanitary conditions but was about ritual purity. Animals with divided hoofs and cleft feet that chewed the cud were considered clean. Only fish with fins and scales were acceptable. According to Douglas the reasoning may have been as follows: fish have fins and scales; shrimp are fish (or at least they swim around in the water like fish), but shrimp don't have fins and scales; therefore shrimp are unclean, or in modern terminology "unnatural." Everything has a place and an order. Mixing things up confuses God's design. Things that don't fit the system are to be avoided, which is probably why mixing different kinds of seed in the same field, cross-breeding animals, or wearing mixed-fiber fabrics was against the code. Such actions disturbed the order of things. Even the way the prohibition against homosexual activity is framed, prohibiting a man from literally "the lying of a woman" (NRSV: "as with a woman") suggests a strong sense of strictly defined or ordered gender-based sexual roles[20] that is consistent with this understanding of the Holiness Code.

In her latest book, Douglas suggests that Leviticus and all of its laws were structured to mirror the tabernacle, the Hebrews' movable worship center.[21] Jacob Milgrom provides a different perspective, proposing that the purity system is rooted in concerns about life and death. For example, blood is necessary for life

---

18. Mary Douglas, *Purity and Danger: An Analysis of the Concepts of Pollution and Taboo* (London: Routledge, 1966).

19. Jacob Milgrom, *Leviticus 1–16*, Anchor Bible (New York: Doubleday, 1991), 61–63.

20. Nissinen, *Homoeroticism*, 45.

21. Mary Douglas, *Leviticus as Literature* (Oxford: Oxford University Press, 1999).

(Leviticus 17:11); thus, its discharge is dangerous. This outlook may account for the taboo on sexual intercourse with a menstruating woman.[22] An additional problem may have been the wasting of the male semen on a woman who was not fertile. At this point choosing between the various views is not possible. The reality may have, at one time or another, involved all of these perspectives.

The prohibitions set forth in Leviticus were serious violations from an ancient point of view, as serious as using dishonest weights, stealing, or adultery (which was understood as an offense against a woman's husband, never against a husband's wife). Thus the ancient Hebrews probably would not have understood the postbiblical division of sin into cultic and moral. For them all violations were serious. The death penalty is prescribed both for mediums and wizards on the one hand (Lev. 20:27) and for those who committed adultery on the other (Lev. 20:10), though the former received the harsher penalty of death by stoning.

The law prohibiting male homosexual intercourse is sandwiched between the law prohibiting the sacrifice of children to the god Molech (Lev. 18:21) and the law prohibiting bestiality (Lev. 18:23). These three laws seem to share a common concern: the wasting of life.[23] In the first case a child who has already been born is killed. In the second case, the antihomosexuality provision, a man wastes his semen in a setting where life cannot be created. This concern is also seen in the story of Onan spilling his seed when he mates with Tamar, his dead brother's widow. Because of this evil deed, God kills Onan (Gen. 38:8–10).

---

22. Milgrom, *Leviticus*, 42–51.

23. Dana Nolan Fewell and David M. Gunn (*Gender, Power, Promise: The Subject of the Bible's First Story* [Nashville: Abingdon Press, 1993], 106) suggest that the unifying theme of all of Leviticus 18 is the disposition of male seed; Melcher ("The Holiness Code," 98–99) sees the Holiness Code in its entirety as concerned with "the protection of the system of patrilineal land tenure, purity of descent, the special status of the priests, and dwelling securely in the land." She views the antihomosexuality provisions, along with the rules against sacrificing children to Molech and against bestiality, as "unproductive" within this overall system.

In the third law, against bestiality, two concerns are perhaps intertwined. In the case of a male, semen is wasted in a context where no life can be created. However, this issue is not present when a woman is involved. The additional concern that exists when either a man or a woman is involved in bestiality is that the proper order from an ancient perspective has been violated. Just as cross-breeding animals was not allowed (Lev. 19:19), so humans and animals were not supposed to mate.

A sense of violation of the natural order may also have been part of the concern in the law prohibiting male homosexual intercourse. Perhaps such activity was considered unnatural because no children could be produced. In an ancient agrarian society, where reproduction was probably understood as the primary and overriding purpose of sexual intercourse (since many children were needed for the survival of the community), that problem was serious, as discussed previously.

In modern Western society the ancient desire not to waste semen is no longer relevant. Overpopulation rather than underpopulation is the challenge. This ancient concern, if taken seriously today, would preclude any form of birth control. In addition, the modern understanding of the biological order of nature is much more sophisticated than that of the ancient Hebrews. Thus, cross-breeding animals is not offensive. Most moderns do share a reverence for life that makes repugnant the idea of sacrificing a child, and bestiality disgusts all but the most kinky. Apparently the ancient Hebrews felt this way about the various behaviors labeled unclean in the Bible.

Thus, although modernity — including most faith traditions — rejects the ancient Hebrew concern for wasting of semen and premodern understandings of the order of nature, the principle of reverence for life is affirmed not only in religious communities but also by societies at large as reflected in legal systems. To the extent that the Hebrew laws grow out of this broad concern, they continue to be valid. Since the antihomosexuality rules appear to have developed out of culturally limited concerns, considering these laws as outdated and no longer valid might seem appropriate. Christians and many Jews treat in this manner many of the violations described in Leviticus, both those specifically rejected in the New Testament and others that are not mentioned. If homosexuality were not explicitly addressed in the New Testament, that approach would be logical. Because several New Testament passages deal with the subject, however, these texts need to be considered before a final judgment can be made.

Homosexuality in the Cult?

Several additional biblical texts are perhaps references to homosexual behavior in a worship setting (Deut. 23:18; 1 Kgs. 14:24; 15:12; 22:46; 2 Kgs. 23:7; Job 36:14). Found in these texts are two terms that are difficult to understand, but which are often thought to refer to male and female cult prostitutes. Whether these Hebrew terms *qedesh* and *qedesha* had any sexual connotation is not certain, nor is whether the people involved received money for their services. The terms are derived from the Hebrew root meaning "holy" and refer to some sort of temple functionaries, but the Bible does not define their precise roles. Although biblical scholars have traditionally assumed that they were cult prostitutes based primarily on parallels in other ancient Near Eastern and Greek literature, the evidence is weak and contemporary scholars are less confident in their assertions on this matter.[24]

Noah, Ham, and Canaan

In Genesis 9:22–25, Noah gets drunk and lies down naked in his tent. His son Ham sees him in this condition. The other sons

---

24. See Nissinen, *Homoeroticism*, 41; Phyllis A. Bird, "The Bible in Christian Ethical Deliberation concerning Homosexuality: Old Testament Contributions," in *Homosexuality, Science, and the "Plain" Sense of Scripture*, ed. David L. Balch (Grand Rapids: Eerdmans, 2000), 60–62 [142–76]; Tikva Frymer-Kensky, *In the Wake of the Goddesses: Women, Culture, and the Biblical Transformation of Pagan Myth* (New York: Fawcett Columbine, 1992), 199–202; Bernhard W. Anderson, *Understanding the Old Testament*, abridged 4th ed. (Upper Saddle River, N.J.: Prentice-Hall, 1998), 169; Mordechai Cogan and Hayim Tadmor, *II Kings*, Anchor Bible (New York: Doubleday, 1988), 286.

respond by walking backward toward their father with a blanket to cover his nakedness without looking at him. The phrase "uncover the nakedness of..." is a euphemism for sexual relations (see Leviticus 18:6–19). Although Ham does not uncover his father's nakedness but merely sees it, the fact that his brothers re-cover their father and that Noah, upon wakening, realizes not simply that he has been seen but that something has been *done* to him, suggests that the meaning of "see the nakedness of" here is the same as "uncover the nakedness of" in Leviticus 18. When Noah wakes up and finds out what his youngest son did to him (apparently homosexual incest and rape), he curses Canaan. Some confusion in the text exists over the identity of the third son. Japheth is introduced as Noah's third and presumably youngest son in Genesis 10:1, but Ham — who is introduced in Genesis 10:1 second — is the one who sees Noah naked. In Genesis 9:24–25, the tradition seems to be that Canaan was the youngest son. Probably different versions of the story have been combined. In any case Shem, Ham, and Japheth represent the three divisions of humanity from an ancient Hebrew perspective (essentially Semites, Africans, and Europeans). Canaan is cursed because the Hebrews viewed themselves as distinct from and superior to their near Canaanite neighbors. Whether the Canaanites were given to homosexual relations either in general or in the cult is unclear (see above). What seems likely, however, is that the Hebrews used this brush to tar their enemies.

The negative depiction in this story of the Canaanites through the character Canaan fits in with the presentation of the residents of Sodom, a Canaanite town, trying to homosexually rape the men whom Lot has taken into his house (Genesis 19). The incestuous aspect of the story of Noah, Ham, and Canaan is also in line with the narrative of Lot's daughters' getting their father drunk and then raping him and incestuously conceiving the two nations of Ammon and Moab, both Canaanite kingdoms (Genesis 19:31–38). Just as the story of Sodom does not provide much help in deciding the Bible's attitude toward homosexual relationships between consenting adults, neither does this tale of the homosexual incestuous rape of Noah.

David and Jonathan, Ruth and Naomi

The friendships between David and Jonathan and between Ruth and Naomi are sometimes interpreted as involving a homosexual element. Nothing in the text of either of these stories, however, explicitly suggests that the characters had sexual relations with one another. Such a possibility is not preposterous, especially in the case of David and Jonathan, but if true the narrators chose to exclude this aspect of the relationships, and these stories therefore can hardly be used as strong evidence of a positive attitude toward homosexual behavior.

Summary of Passages in the Hebrew Scriptures

Of all the texts in the Hebrew Scriptures considered above, only the Levitical proscription of male homosexual intercourse and the prescribed punishment, death, unambiguously bear on the question of whether homosexual intercourse between consenting adults is morally acceptable. Since these texts only deal with males, nothing in the Hebrew Scriptures relates directly to the question of lesbianism. Of the two relevant Levitical texts, most interpreters focus on Leviticus 18:22, the proscription, and largely ignore Leviticus 20:13, the death penalty. However, logic would suggest that if one of these two texts is taken seriously, the other one should be considered with equal gravity.[25] Although many Christians reject homosexuality, at least partly based on Leviticus 18:22, very few believe that offenders should be executed; people who act on such notions are prosecuted as murderers in the United States and generally viewed as dangerous lunatics. We return to Leviticus 18:22 after considering the New Testament passages.

New Testament Teaching on Homosexuality

The three New Testament texts that are generally considered to deal with homosexuality are 1 Corinthians 6:9, 1 Timothy 1:10,

---

25. Seow, "A Heterotextual Perspective," 15.

and Romans 1:26–27. In 1 Corinthians 6:9, Paul begins by asking a rhetorical question: "Do you not know that wrongdoers will not inherit the kingdom of God?" What follows is a list of the kinds of sinful people who will be excluded: thieves, greedy people, drunks, revilers, robbers, and several terms designating sexual offenders. After adulterers and idolaters — a group sometimes linked with the sexually immoral (see Rom. 1:26) — comes the Greek *malakoi,* literally "soft," but often meaning effeminate and sometimes used in Hellenistic times for the passive (anal-receptive) partner of a male homosexual couple. English versions of the Bible have translated *malakoi* in a variety of ways. Many interpreters have argued that Paul may have coined the following term, *arsenokoitai,* from Leviticus 18:22 for males (*arsen*) lying with males (as with a woman), i.e., the active role.[26] The NRSV translates "sodomites" in this manner. Translations of this word, however, have varied dramatically over the centuries. Following Robin Scroggs,[27] the NRSV translates *malakoi* as "male prostitutes," which is within the range of the meanings of the term but is not the required translation.

Dale Martin analyzes the uses of *arsenokoitai* in the contexts where it occurs outside the Bible and concludes that although the term may refer to homosexual sex, it may also refer more generally to some form of exploitation involving sex, not even necessarily homosexual sex.[28] If *arsenokoitai* did mean the active homosexual partner, then *malakoi* would most sensibly be understood in its restricted meaning of the passive member. If, however, *arsenokoitai* refers to people who engage in some type of sexual exploitation, which seems likely, then *malakoi* could be understood in its more general meaning of effeminate (note the misogyny implied in the negative connotations of the term).[29] In terms of accuracy, a better translation of the two terms is as sexual ex-

26. Robin Scroggs, *The New Testament and Homosexuality* (Philadelphia: Fortress Press, 1983), 85–86.

27. Ibid., 62–65, 106.

28. Dale B. Martin, "*Arsenokoites* and *Malakos:* Meanings and Consequences," in Brawley, ed. *Biblical Ethics and Homosexuality,* 118–23.

29. See also Nissinen, *Homoeroticism,* 117–18.

ploiters and effeminate, despite the politically incorrect nature of the latter word.

Although the exact meaning of the terms *arsenokoitai* and *malakoi* may not be absolutely clear, Paul's main point is obviously the impropriety of civil lawsuits for Christians. Ironically Christians often focus on the impropriety that Paul mentions in passing — *malakoi* and *arsenokoitai*, the precise definitions of which are elusive — and ignore the impropriety that Paul was admonishing his readers to avoid, about which no ambiguity is possible! Contemporary Christians sue each other in civil courts without regard to Paul's undeniable warning. How can Christians take seriously what he comments on in passing, even assuming the definitions of the words are clear, and not take seriously his main point?[30]

Another vice list, in 1 Timothy 1:10, includes various kinds of murderers (1 Tim. 1:9), fornicators (or male prostitutes?), and *arsenokoitai*, which the NRSV again translates as "sodomites." The list concludes with slave traders (perhaps a reference to the trade of sexual slaves),[31] liars, and perjurers. The fact that *arsenokoitai* is followed by slave traders, a group who exploited others, adds weight to Martin's evidence for *arsenokoitai* as sexual exploiters of some sort, since the vices in the lists were often grouped according to their similarity to other vices in the list.

Romans 1:26–27 is the most important of the New Testament passages dealing specifically with homosexuality because 1:27 undoubtedly deals with male homosexual practice and both verses include information about why Paul found certain types of sexual behavior objectionable. Nevertheless, v. 26, quoted here, is not as obvious in one regard as is usually thought:

> For this reason [idolatry] God gave them up to degrading passions. Their women [literally females] exchanged natural intercourse for unnatural.

30. Seow, "Textual Orientation," 25.
31. Scroggs, *The New Testament and Homosexuality*, 120.

This verse is probably the one explicit reference to lesbianism in the entire Bible. The fact that it is followed by v. 27, which un-ambiguously refers to male homosexuality, suggests to the vast majority of modern readers that the kind of unnatural intercourse to which the author refers in v. 26 is same-sex intercourse between women. That reading is not the only possible interpretation of this verse, however.

Contemporary Westerners tend to think of gay and lesbian sex as two sides of the same coin, but in the ancient world this pairing is not as obvious. Although Paul is possibly referring to lesbian-ism, plausibly what he has in mind are other "unnatural" types of intercourse, e.g., women taking the "active" role. Thus, that the Bible has anything to say, at least in an explicit fashion, about lesbianism is not certain.[32] Nevertheless, research by Bernadette Brooten on lesbianism in the ancient world indicates that Romans 1:26 probably is a reference to consensual lesbian relationships.[33] The concern was probably that the ancients considered women taking the active part in sexual relations as an unnatural gender boundary crossing.

The next verse, Romans 1:27, reads:

> …and in the same way also the men, giving up natural intercourse with women [literally females], were consumed with passion for one another. Men [literally males] commit-ted shameless acts with men [literally males] and received in their own persons the due penalty for their error.

Paul suggests here that a result of Gentile idolatry (Rom. 1:25) is male homosexual intercourse, a result that he apparently viewed as deplorable.

Paul may have thought male homosexual intercourse was unnatural for the same reasons that many of the behaviors pro-scribed in the Holiness Code were perhaps thought unclean: They

---

32. James Miller, "The Practices of Romans 1:26: Homosexual or Heterosexual," *Novum Testamentum* 37 (1995): 1–11; P. J. Tomson, *Paul and the Jewish Law: Halakha in the Letters of the Apostle to the Gentiles,* Compendia rerum judicarum ad Novum Testamentum 3.1 (Assen: Van Gorcum; Minneapolis: Fortress, 1990), 94, n. 157.

33. Bernadette J. Brooten, *Love between Women: Early Christian Responses to Female Homoeroticism* (Chicago: University of Chicago Press, 1996).

were probably believed to confuse the created order. Paul's use of the term "male," *arsenes*, rather than the more general term "man," *anthropos*, is reminiscent of the antihomosexuality law in Leviticus 18:22, where the Hebrew for male, *zakar*, is also used.[34] If Paul did use the term with the Holiness Code in mind, this usage could fit in well with his description of homosexual behavior as unnatural, raising the issue of whether a kind of nascent natural law is present in Paul's thought. The answer is probably yes.[35] However, Paul's understanding of nature was quite different from contemporary Western ideas on the subject. For him a man wearing long hair was unnatural (1 Cor. 11:14). For us that state would seem more natural than hair that has been shortened by scissors or razor. Ancient conceptualizations of the laws of nature evidently had as much to do with what was conventional as with what we today would consider inherent in human biology.

If Paul is upholding Leviticus 18:22, as seems likely, this support might seem to be at odds with Paul's somewhat negative attitude toward the Mosaic law. Nevertheless, he was not antinomian. He believed that Christians were to be holy and pure and thus distinguishable from pagans in a similar fashion as Jews were to keep themselves separate from Gentiles.[36] The difference was that the distinctively Jewish provisions of the law, such as kosher rules, circumcision, and other regulations, were no longer in force. Paul may have believed that the proscription of homosexual behavior that was a part of the Jewish law was not specifically Jewish, but had more general applicability.[37] If so, no logical conflict would exist between his rejection

---

34. Richard B. Hays, "Relations Natural and Unnatural: A Response to John Boswell's Exegesis of Romans 1," *Journal of Religious Ethics* 14, no. 1 (spring 1986): 184–215.

35. Joseph Fitzmyer, *Romans*, Anchor Bible (New York: Doubleday, 1992), 128–29, 273–75.

36. Jerome H. Neyrey, *Paul, in Other Words: A Cultural Reading of His Letters* (Louisville, Ky.: Westminster/John Knox Press, 1994).

37. Helmut Koester ("Physis" in *Theological Dictionary of the New Testament*, vol. 9, ed. Gerhard Friedrich, trans. Geoffrey W. Bromiley [Grand Rapids: Eerdmans, 1974], 273) writes that the stress on sexual faults corresponds to the so-called Noahic commandments of rabbinic Judaism (the commandments thought to apply to all humanity).

of kosher regulations and circumcision and his upholding of the antihomosexuality prohibition.

Influences Shaping Paul's Views on Homosexuality

Paul was a Jew. Therefore first considering his views on homosexuality within the context of Jewish tradition makes good sense. Paul was also an educated Roman citizen, so another way to understand Paul's attitude toward homosexuality is to examine his views in light of the prevailing attitudes in the Greco-Roman world he inhabited. Beginning in the sixth century B.C.E., homosexual love became a prominent part of Greek society. The most common form was pederasty, a sexual relationship between an older man and a younger one, typically an adolescent. In the first century C.E., some moralists in the Greco-Roman world were still practicing and advocating the traditional kind of pederasty, though typically without the pedagogical focus that had marked the ancient Greek practice. Some evidence, however, suggests that at the time Paul wrote Romans, pederastic practices were waning while other forms of homosexual behavior continued,[38] which would not be inconsistent with continuing critiques of pederastic practices. Often the peak of negative comments on a subject comes when the problem is beginning to disappear. In addition, practices may continue to shape cultural thinking on a matter long after those practices have subsided.

Forms of homosexuality other than pederasty, such as the sexual exploitation of young male slaves and the voluntary sale of sex by young male prostitutes to older male patrons, may have become more common than pederasty during the first century C.E. and were often condemned. Seneca, a Stoic philosopher, hated feminized male slaves and their owners who were involved in general debauchery. Plutarch, a Greek moralist, believed pederasty was against nature and advocated marriage between a man and a woman, both for procreation and affection.[39] Dio Chrysostom

---

38. Mark Smith, "Ancient Bisexuality and the Interpretation of Romans 1:26–27," *Journal of the American Academy of Religion* 64 (1996): 223–95.
39. Nissinen, *Homoeroticism*, 84–85.

taught the ideas and values of both the Cynics and the Stoics. He
saw homosexuality as essentially exploitative, and he also viewed
it as the result of insatiable lust. He believed that men who had
had their fill of sex with women, especially women prostitutes,
would then turn to men.[40] Thus, what had originated at its best
as a pedagogical, spiritual relationship between an older and a
younger man, which also usually involved homosexual relations,
evolved into what the Gentile moralists believed was a lustful,
exploitative homosexual relationship in which the pedagogical
and spiritual elements had largely disappeared. David Fredrickson points out that the Gentile moralists viewed *eros* — erotic
passion, whether homosexual or heterosexual — as dangerous as
it leads to loss of self-control, which in turn results in unjust actions. This distaste for sexual passion fits in with Paul's broader
point that God gave idolaters up to their own lust and degrading
passion.[41]

In general Greco-Roman philosophers in the first century c.e.
criticized homosexual behavior as unnatural for two reasons.
First, such activity did not lead to procreation. Second, homosexual practices involved gender role reversal. Moralists especially
disliked what they viewed as the effeminate, non-manly passive
partner. In addition, they were concerned about the exploitative
nature of prostitution, both homosexual and heterosexual.[42] Paul
may have been especially open to contemporary Gentile Greco-
Roman ideas about homosexuality, which dovetail nicely with the
traditional Jewish aversion to homosexual practice.[43]

The views of Hellenistic Jews were similar to their Gentile
counterparts. Philo viewed homosexuality as violating the order
of nature and as a result of lust.[44] Both Philo's and Josephus's

---

40. Furnish, *The Moral Teaching of Paul,* 62–63; G. Mussies, *Dio Chrysostom and the New Testament,* Studia ad Corpus Hellenisticum Novi Testamenti, 2 (Leiden: E. J. Brill, 1972), 138–39.

41. David E. Fredrickson, "Natural and Unnatural Use in Romans 1:24–27," in *Homosexuality, Science, and the "Plain Sense" of Scripture,* ed. David L. Balch (Grand Rapids: Eerdmans, 2000), 197–222.

42. Nissinen, *Homoeroticism,* 87–88.

43. David F. Greenberg, *The Construction of Homosexuality* (Chicago: University of Chicago Press, 1988), 215–16.

44. Furnish, *The Moral Teaching of Paul,* 64–65.

comments on the story of Sodom and Gomorrah are interesting in this regard. Although nothing in the biblical story suggests that Lot's guests were particularly youthful or handsome, Philo (*On Abraham; Questions and Answers on Genesis 4:37*) and Josephus (*Jewish Antiquities* I, 194–204) interpret the story as if these characteristics were present, thus suggesting that for them pederasty was the typical way homosexuality expressed itself and the form of homosexuality that they took for granted. Philo's interpretation of the Levitical antihomosexuality laws (*Special Laws* III, 37) also narrows the focus to pederasty.

Paul's issue was not simply a moral one. Paul links pagan, Gentile idolatry and homosexual behavior, a connection that may also dovetail with ancient Hebrew perspectives. Hosea was the first Hebrew prophet to liken the apostasy of his people to an adulterous affair. Whether he was accusing the people of participating in sexual rites in worship or simply using the imagery of adultery as a means of driving home the shame of their worshiping other gods is unclear. Jeremiah and Ezekiel followed in Hosea's footsteps in utilizing sexual imagery to shock their listeners into horror at their abandonment of God. The Apocryphal book of the Wisdom of Solomon makes the same linkage:

> For the idea of making idols was the beginning of fornication and the invention of them was the corruption of life. (14:12)

Of course, Paul is saying something more than that idolatry is like immoral sexual behavior. He says that idolatry leads to unnatural sexual practices. The connection between Hellenistic idolatry and homosexual practice may not simply have been on an abstract level — that is, worshiping the wrong god resulting in sex with the wrong partner or in the wrong manner. Perhaps the connection was practical as well. In other words, Paul may have been concerned about homosexual practices in Gentile pagan worship.

Given its context, the homosexuality that is condemned in the Holiness Code may have been practiced in Canaanite worship, or at least the Hebrews may have thought it was (see discussion above). A similar concern could be involved in the book of Romans, where homosexual behavior is attributed to idolatry. The reason the homosexual behavior is viewed negatively would still be the perception of its unnaturalness, but the type of behavior at issue might have been limited to or at least focused on pagan worship practices.

Philo's concern was with the honored presence of the effeminate male prostitute in the Greek cults (*Special Laws*). The religious traditions of the Romans, largely inherited from the Greeks, included few legal limitations (practically speaking) on sexual behavior. As a result the pagans were known for their sexual debauchery. Sexual rites were incorporated into religious practices.[45] Sexual elements probably existed in the initiations of the mystery religions, though the evidence is not unambiguous. In the Dionysian cults, however, sexuality was less veiled. Real sexual intercourse occurred, particularly pederastic forms.[46] Thus Paul may have perceived that sex in general and pederastic forms of it in particular were virtually a substitute for religion. Sex is such a powerful force that this kind of confusion is not hard to understand.

Although Paul does not explicitly limit his condemnation of homosexuality to exploitative and/or cultic forms, his view of homosexual behavior may have been so colored by these manifestations, as well as the contemporary philosophical and ancient Jewish beliefs that homosexuality was unnatural, that imagining a homosexual partnership between equals would have been difficult for him. Thus Paul may have condemned all forms of male and most likely female homosexual behavior *as he understood them,* because of traditional Jewish and contemporary Jewish and Gentile philosophical concerns about unnaturalness, contemporary criticism of his time of the lustful and therefore exploitative nature of much homosexual activity, and its connection with ancient and first century C.E. pagan worship.

Before leaving this passage, another kind of context beyond the religious and cultural ones is worth considering. In Romans

---

45. James B. DeYoung, "The Meaning of 'Nature' in Romans 1 and Its Implications," *Journal of the Evangelical Theological Society* 31, no. 4 (December 1988): 436.

46. Walter Burkert, John Raffan, trans., *Creation of the Sacred: Tracks of Biology in Early Religions* (Cambridge: Harvard University Press, 1985), 109.

Paul is dialoguing with an imaginary Jewish Christian who would probably have found homosexuality repugnant, as Paul himself no doubt did. By focusing on forms`of sexual behavior that his Jewish audience would have reviled, Paul prepares for the next stage of his argument. The Jews to whom he spoke could easily agree with the idea that homosexual intercourse was the result of the pagans' idolatrous religions. Paul goes on in Romans 1:28–32 to catalogue the pagans' sins in a way that makes the vice lists in 1 Corinthians 6:9 and 1 Timothy 1:10 appear mild in comparison.

In Romans 2 Paul proceeds to tell his Jewish audience that when they judge the pagans, they condemn themselves because they are essentially doing the very same things (Rom. 2:1)! He is not saying that they too are involved in "unnatural" sex but that their sins are the moral equivalent. He is chastising them for their arrogance, much as Jesus says that every married person who has lusted after someone other than his or her spouse has in effect committed adultery (Matt. 5:28) and complains about people who would remove the speck in someone else's eye without noting the beam in their own eye (Matt. 7:3–5; Luke 6:41–42). In turn Paul's concern to foster an awareness of sinfulness in Jewish Christians was intended to make them understand that their salvation did not rely on their own goodness, but rather on God's grace. This rhetorical context is important in the broader consideration of the Bible and homosexuality.

Applying Hermeneutical Principles to Biblical Texts

Having reviewed the relevant biblical passages, we need now to see where we are. Of all the biblical verses considered, the only ones that may reasonably be interpreted as contributing to the debate about homosexual intercourse between freely consenting adults are Leviticus 18:22 and 20:13, 1 Corinthians 6:9, 1 Timothy 1:10, and Romans 1:26–27. First, one possible conclusion is that the antihomosexuality law in Leviticus 18:22 should not be rejected out of hand, on the grounds that Paul's words on the matter in Romans 1:27, which denounce male homosexual behavior as understood at the time, uphold it. The punishment in Leviticus 20:13 can be ignored because the New Testament does not uphold it. Second, although the evidence is not definitive, nevertheless the New Testament passages of 1 Corinthians 6:9 and 1 Timothy 1:10 may be understood — and Romans 1:27 should be interpreted — as dealing broadly with male homosexual behavior *in its cultural context*. Third, Romans 1:26 should similarly be interpreted as a reference to the female homosexual practice of the time. Finally, we should give weight to these texts because they deal with forms of homosexual practice that are related to contemporary behavior, even though the conceptualizations of gender roles and human sexuality in general have changed over time. These passages, however, should not be accepted or rejected simply because on a gut level we like or dislike them.

At this point we consider these passages in light of the hermeneutical principle introduced in chapter 2, which was gleaned from the study of the history of the way biblical interpreters have responded to scientific advances. The Bible is not authoritative in matters of science. When the evidence mounts for a new scientific perspective that seems to conflict with biblical teaching, sensitive readers should begin to reevaluate that teaching (see chapter 2). Specifically, the scientific evidence now suggests in some instances a genetic basis for homosexuality; in other words, homosexuality is, at least for some people, natural rather than unnatural (see chapter 1).

The most important of all the passages we have considered is Romans 1:26–27. Paul's suggestion here that homosexual passion and behavior are unnatural may have been a result in part of his Jewish heritage and in part of the moral philosophy of his day, which also viewed homosexuality as unnatural. The reasons that Paul thought homosexuality was unnatural do not much matter. The fact is that he apparently did. Admittedly, his conceptualization of nature was different from our own — prescientific and culturally bound, which is not to say that contemporary conceptualizations are without cultural bias. Twenty-first-century biology suggests that Paul's view of homosexuality as unnatural was wrong. Christians no more need to follow him here than we need to accept the biblical notion that the earth is flat or that the sun revolves around the earth. In addition, traditional hermeneutical principles are helpful. Since the Hebrew Scriptures are read in light of the New Testament, the Epistles in light of the Gospels, and specific advice or comments in light of more generally enunciated principles, we move now to a consideration of these passages in light of the New Testament's overall teaching on law with the greatest weight going to Jesus' perspective.

The antihomosexuality rules in Leviticus, the possible references to male homosexuality in 1 Corinthians 6:9 and 1 Timothy 1:10, the probable reference to female homosexuality in Romans 1:26, and the one irrefutable reference to male homosexuality (whether more broadly or more narrowly construed) in Romans 1:27 are examples of specific advice. Although they are not explicitly contrary to the spirit of Jesus' teaching on law or other general teaching on law in the New Testament, neither do they carry the same weight as the overarching principle that emerges from all the New Testament authors. This principle of a mindful, heartfelt, and spiritual approach to determining what God requires entrusts contemporary people of faith with the solemn responsibility and the freedom to reinterpret specific laws or advice in certain cases, as Jesus, Peter, and Paul themselves did. Combining this principle with the one propounded in chapter 2 — that scientific advances that conflict or seem to conflict with biblical texts should move Christian interpreters to reinterpret texts — the result is a mandate to consider contemporary evidence on the subject of human sexuality.

This approach provides a reasonable way to take the Bible seriously without accepting its generally negative attitude toward homosexuality. Concluding that contemporary Christians need not heed the specific biblical injunctions against homosexual behavior, however, is not enough. Two additional steps are crucial. First, thoughtful interpreters should reflect on the biblical teaching that accompanies one of the antihomosexuality texts, Romans 1:26–27. Here Paul challenges a nonsexual kind of sinful behavior that is endemic within many Christian communities. Second, broader biblical perspectives that may affect ethical judgments about homosexuality may deepen our viewpoint.

New Testament Teaching on Judgment

Because Paul's words about homosexuality in Romans 1 are in a passage where the main purpose is to criticize judgmental, self-righteous Jews, and because Jesus also had important things to say about judgment, we consider these passages briefly. Jesus' words are quite familiar:

> Do not judge, so that you may not be judged. For with the judgment you make you will be judged, and the measure you give will be the measure you get. Why do you see the speck in your neighbor's eye, but do not notice the log in your own eye? Or how can you say to your neighbor, 'Let me take the speck out of your eye,' while the log is in your own eye? You hypocrite, first take the log out of your own eye, and then you will see clearly to take the speck out of your neighbor's eye. (Matt. 7:1–5; Luke 6:37–38, 41–42; Mark 4:24)

The point here is that people should be slow to judge others because their own sins may well be greater. A similar point is made in the story about the woman caught in adultery (John 7:53–8:11). Jesus is not saying that judgments should never be made, which is evident from the passage that follows the one about specks and logs in Matthew:

> Do not give what is holy to dogs; and do not throw your pearls before swine, or they will trample them under foot and turn and maul you. (Matt. 7:6)

People of faith make judgments all the time as individuals, and congregations also are called on to determine who should and should not be in positions of leadership. Nevertheless, we all should be aware of our own shortcomings in judging others and not be harsher on others than an impartial judge would be with them.

Following Jesus' lead in Romans 1–2, Paul criticizes his fellow Jews who are quick to condemn their Gentile brothers and sisters for their lapses. From Paul's perspective the accusers are no better than the accused and thus are doubly condemned. Applying this text to the subject at hand, Paul in effect is saying to heterosexuals that before homosexuals are condemned for their behavior, an inner stock taking is in order. Ironically many contemporary Christians take Paul's words on homosexuality, about which there is some lack of clarity, more seriously than his primary concern about judgment, a concern that is unambiguous!

Reflections on the Bible's Teaching on Sexuality

Should the Bible's general (negative) attitude toward homosexuality be retained? The approach outlined above suggests not. But to reject the negative attitude about homosexuality does not necessarily imply the acceptability of all homosexual behavior. Rather, such a new approach simply removes the negative statements as evidence to be used in contemporary moral arguments. Christians should still examine positive biblical principles in considering the kinds of sexual relationships, whether homosexual or heterosexual, that may be morally normative today.

Genesis 2:24, the statement about a man leaving his parents and clinging to his wife, and Jesus' citing of this verse and adding his own statement that what has been brought together should not be torn apart, suggest a model of lifelong partnership in which develops an intimacy so profound that two individuals on some level become a unity.

As has been discussed above, this prescription does not mean that everyone must marry, nor does the command to the first humans to be fruitful and multiply require that all humans reproduce. Nor is the only form of sexual union necessarily heterosexual. Male-female union is the most common pattern and surely the preferred pattern in a rural agrarian society where many laborers are needed, but not the only pattern.

Beyond the rules in the Hebrew Scriptures about which relatives are allowed to marry which relatives, some of which concur with contemporary practice and some of which do not, the Bible also includes rules against adultery and fornication. In the Hebrew Scriptures, adultery is defined as sexual intercourse between a married woman and a man. A married man having sexual relations with a prostitute does not commit adultery, at least not according to the Hebrew Scriptures. These rules portrayed women as virtually the property of their husbands. Adultery was thus seen as a crime against the husband. Similarly, rape, for which no exact term exists in the Hebrew vocabulary, offended the woman's husband or father rather than the woman. Jesus broadened the adultery rules to such a degree that virtually every married person has committed this sin. What to do?

The New Testament teaching on law suggests that Christians should look to the Bible and the Spirit for guidance in developing a sensible contemporary ethic, keeping in mind the model of life-long partnership as an important ideal. Without trying to answer all the questions involved in sexual ethics, the focus here is on the matter of the propriety of homosexual relationships. Since the model presented in Genesis 2:24 does not mandate heterosexual pairing, seemingly that verse can provide a model for lifelong homosexual partnerships as much as for heterosexual ones. The goal is the same — intimacy developed over a lifetime.

Gifts from Conflict

The conflict between the understanding of human sexuality that is emerging from contemporary science and the traditional interpretation of the Bible's teaching on the matter of homosexuality is a gift, forcing people who revere the Bible to reexamine it with new eyes. The search for an approach that would reconcile the findings of contemporary biology and the teaching of the Bible may bring today's Bible readers closer to the *way* biblical authors thought or interpreted scripture than was previously understood even if it widens the gap between modern perspectives on sexuality. Each generation reads the same scriptures and yet does not exhaust their interpretive possibilities. New issues and concerns force a reexamination of the texts, which sometimes results in a major paradigm shift. Whenever people grow too comfortable with their understanding of the Bible, new developments arise that call people of faith to wrestle. Like Jacob, we may emerge limping, but with a blessing.

SCRIPTURE INDEX

GENERAL INDEX

Draper, J. W., 46, 69
Drees, William B., 70n
Dreyer, J. L. E., 49n, 51n
Dupree, Hunter, 68n
earth, shape of, 9, 46–51, 119
Ebers, George, 25, 25n
Edwards, James R., 94, 94n
ego-dystonic homosexuality, 42
environment, 21, 23, 28–30, 37–41
epistatic gene, 22–23
Epperson, Susan, 73
Erdokimov, P., 14n
eunuch, 84–85
evolution, 46, 68–75
experimental design, 38–39
expressivity, 21–23, 37
Ezekiel, 115
family studies, 28
fertilization, 31, 40
Fewell, Dana Nolan, 104n
Field, P. M., 33, 34n
Fields, Weston W., 96n
Fitzmyer, Joseph, 112n
Fleishmann, Albert, 73
fornication, 82, 121
Foscarini, Paolo Antonio, 63–64
Fredrickson, David E., 114, 114n
Friedman, R. C., 29n
Friedrich, Gerhard, 112n
Frymer-Kensky, Tikva, 106n
Fulker, D. W., 23n
fundamentalist, 72
Furnish, Victor Paul, 95, 95n, 99n, 114n
Gasztonyi, Z., 27–28, 28n
gay gene, 8, 23–24, 37
gender, 30–31
gene, 20, 23; epistatic, 22–23; gay, 23–24, 37; interaction, 28; multiple gene control, 22, 25, 37; pleiomorphic, 22; recessive, 21, 27–28; redundant, 22; sex-linked, 21–22, 27–28
Gaiser, J. Frederick, 85n, 90n, 92n
Galileo, 52n, 53n, 58–65, 68–69
Gamba, Marina, 59
gap theory, 67
genetics, 8, 20–25
genome, 40
gentiles, 87, 98, 101, 111–12, 114–16
geocentrism, 9, 46–47, 52–53, 59, 119
geology, 9, 47, 65–67
Gibeah, 96, 100
Goethe, 38–39, 39n
Goodfellow, P., 40n
Gordon, J. H., 34n
Gorski, R. A., 33n, 34n, 35, 35n, 36n
Gosse, Philip, 67
grace, 87, 117
Gray, Asa, 72
Greek literature, 15
Green, R., 29–30, 29n, 30n
Greenberg, David F., 114n
Gregory, Frederick, 69n, 70n, 71
Gubbay, J., 40n
Gunn, David M., 104n
Gythiel, A. P., 14n

Halperin, D. M., 17n
Ham, 79, 106–7
Hamer, D. H., 23–25, 23n, 24n
Hays, Richard B., 97n, 112n
heart, 79–82, 87–89, 119
heliocentrism, 9, 46–47, 53–54, 58–59
Helminiak, D. A., 97n
Hendricks, S. E., 33n
Henslow, John Stevens, 68
heritability, 20, 37, 43
hermeneutics, 49n, 62n, 78, 117–18
Hesselink, I. John, 92n
Heston, L. L., 29n
heterosexuality, 10, 81, 94–95, 114, 121–22
Hettema, C. A., 24n
higher biblical criticism, 68
Hines, M., 34n, 36n
history, 13–15
Hodge, Charles, 71
Hoffman, M. A., 34n, 35n
holiness rules, 80–83, 86–87, 101–3, 111–12, 115
Holloway, R., 35n
Holy Spirit, 64, 76, 87–88, 91, 122
homoerotic, 17–18
hormonal studies, 30–37
Hosea, 115
Houston, L., 35n
Howell, Kenneth, J., 49n, 52n, 54n, 55n, 58n, 61n, 62, 62n, 65n
Hu, N., 23n
Hu, S., 23n, 24, 24n, 25n
Human Genome Project, 22
Hunter, David G., 14n
Hutton, James, 66
Huxley, Thomas, 69
hypothalamus, 18, 35–36
hypothesis, 18, 38, 75
idolatry, 114–17
INAH 2, 36
INAH 3, 35–36
incest, 79, 99n, 107
Indicopleustes, Cosmas, 48
inerrancy, 57
Ingoli, Francesco, 64
inheritance patterns, 22–24
interpretation of scientific results, 16, 37–40, 43
interpretation, principles of, 9–10, 46, 76, 78–92, 93, 119, 122
intersex, 17
Isaiah of Jerusalem, 84
Isidore, Bishop of Seville, 50
Jacob, 123
Japheth, 107
Jeremiah, 10, 95, 115
Jerome, 48
Jesus, 10, 79–83, 86–91, 95–96, 119–21
John of Holywood, 52
Jonathan, 79, 108
Josephus, 99, 114–15
Kallmann, F. J., 26, 26n
Kendler, K. S., 24n
Kepler, Johann, 49n, 55–56, 60
Kertbeny, Karl Maria, 17

Pliny, 50
Plomin, R., 24n
Plutarch, 15, 113
polygamy, 95
Pomeroy, W. B., 27n
Powell, Baden, 68, 70
Prescott, C. A., 24n
prostitute, 106, 108, 113–14, 116
Protestant(ism), 47, 53–54, 56–57, 71, 75, 91
Ptolemy/ Ptolemaic, 52, 62
Puritans, 57
purity rules. *See* holiness rules
Raffan, John, 116n
Rainer, J. D., 29n
Raisman, G., 33, 34n
Ramet, S. P., 15n
rape, 79, 96–97, 99–100, 106, 122
recessive gene, 21, 27–28
reductionism, 37–38
redundant gene, 22
religious right, 43–44
religious views, 13–15, 19, 43–44
repeatability, 18–19
replicability, 19, 23
Rheticus, Georg Joachim, 54–55
Ritschl, Albrecht, 72
Rogers, Jr., E. F., 15, 15n
Roman Catholic(ism), 47, 52–53, 58, 61,70, 75
Roman world, 15
Rottnek, M., 30n
Roubertoux, P. L., 25n
Rudwick, Martin J. S., 66n
Ruth, 79, 85, 108
Sabbath, 81, 84–85
sacred unions of homosexuals, 75
Sacrobosco, 52
sampling, 17–20, 24, 26–27, 29
Satinover, Jeffrey B., 43–44, 44n
Sawyer, John F. A., 80
Schlegel, W. W., 26, 26n
Scopes, John Thomas, 73
screening analysis, 22–23
scripture, authority of, 76
Scroggs, Robin, 109n, 110n
Scullion, John J., 97n
Segal, N. L., 29n
Seneca, 113
Seow, Choon Leong, 90n, 95n, 97n, 99n, 101n, 108n, 110n
Separate Creation, A: The Search for the Biological Origins of Sexual Orientation (Burr), 36
sex-determining region of the Y (SRY), 31, 40
sex differentiation, 31–33
sex-linked gene, 21–22, 27–28
sexual dimorphism, 33–36
Shanas, E., 14n
Shema, 79, 89
Shields, J., 29n
Shryne, J. E., 34n, 36n
Siker, Jeffrey S., 95n, 97n
Simons, E. L., 13n
singleness, 95–96
Smith, C., 29n
Smith, D. W. E., 13n

Smith, Mark, 113n
Soards, Marion, 98n
social science, 31
Sodom, 107
Sodom and Gomorrah, 96–100, 115
sodomite, 109–10
Southam, A. M., 34n
spirit. *See* Holy Spirit
Steadman, V., 14n
Steck, Odil Hannes, 85n
Stephen, Leslie, 72
stereotype behavior, 30
Stevin, Simon, 57
Stoller, R. J., 29n
Stone, Ken, 97n
Strong, A. H., 71
Supreme Court, 73–74
Swaab, D. F., 34n, 35n
Tadmor, Hayim, 106n
Tamar, 104
Taylor, T., 14, 14n
Tellegen, A., 29n
Temple, Frederick, 71
test group, 19
testosterone, 32
Thales, 49n
theory, scientific, 73, 75
Third Isaiah, 83, 85
Tobet, S. A., 34, 34n
Tomson, P. J., 111n
transgenics, 41
transsexualism, 14
transvestitism, 14
Trendler, R., 29n
Trent, Council of, 58, 62–63
truth, 17, 19, 44
twin studies, 25–29, 37
Twins as a Tool of Behavioral Genetics, 29
Ulrichs, 17
unclean. *See* holiness rules
uniformitarianism, 66–67
Ussher, Bishop, 66
Van der Meer, Jitsu M., 49n, 52n
Venerable Bede, 50
Vinovskis, M. A., 14n
Vivian, N., 40n
Voetius, Gisbertus, 57
Waddell, C. E., 25n
Watson, Alan, 80
Westermann, Claus, 97n
Westman, Robert S., 54n
Whalen, R. E., 33n
Whitaker, Richard E., 95, 95n
White, A. C., 46, 69
Whitman, F. L., 27, 27n, 29, 29n
Wilberforce, Samuel, 69–70
Wilkins, John, 57
Wollesen, F., 29n
World Wide Web, 16
worship. *See* cult
Xq28 region, 23–24
Yahr, P., 34, 34n
Zahniser, D. J., 34n
Zuger, B., 29n